S. Noland

Special Sermons, and Analyses of Ten of Our Lord's Parables

S. Noland

Special Sermons, and Analyses of Ten of Our Lord's Parables

ISBN/EAN: 9783744793056

Printed in Europe, USA, Canada, Australia, Japan

Cover: Foto ©Lupo / pixelio.de

More available books at **www.hansebooks.com**

SPECIAL SERMONS,

AND ANALYSES OF

Ten of Our Lord's Parables.

BY THE REV. S. NOLAND,
Of the Kentucky Conference, M. E. Church, South.

NASHVILLE, TENN.:
SOUTHERN METHODIST PUBLISHING HOUSE.
1885.

DEDICATORY.

WITH PRAYERS FOR THEIR WELFARE,

THIS BOOK IS INSCRIBED TO

"THE TRAVELING, SUPERNUMERARY, SUPERANNUATED, AND WORN-OUT PREACHERS, THEIR WIVES, WIDOWS, AND CHILDREN,"

OF THE

Kentucky Conference of the M. E. Church, South,

BY THE AUTHOR.

PREFACE.

Our book contains a sermon by the author in memory of Bishop H. H. Kavanaugh; one on "Good Works;" one on "The Discoveries of Sin;" and one on "The Resurrection of Christ." These four sermons are intermingled with analyses of ten of our Lord's parables, viz.: "The Sower," "The Tares," "The Barren Fig-tree," "The Prodigal and the Self-righteous Son," "The Great Supper," "The Good Samaritan," "The Pharisee and Publican," "The Unjust Judge," "The Wise and Foolish Virgins," and "The Rich Man and Lazarus."

Our Lord declared that he spake in parables to his followers that they might know the mystery of the kingdom of God. He made this statement early in his ministry, and for nearly three years he abounded in this manner of instruction. It is said by the evangelist that without a parable he did not speak to the multitude. No doubt this kind of teaching coming from our Saviour conveys truth to the mind and heart with unusual distinctness and power. The composition of all the parables is exceedingly plain, and without apparent effort at ornament; but the impression produced by them has never been equaled by uninspired human writings. An able advocate once said to an able divine that he could make as good a parable as those attributed to Jesus. The divine gave him two weeks to produce the parable. At the end of the time the advocate reported that he had succeeded in words and style, but had wholly failed to put the soul into it that he found in the parables of Jesus. He started out to discredit the parables of our Lord, but was convinced of their inspiration. Many parables have been written with great care by many men, but they are all destitute of spiritual life. Jesus never wrote a parable, but spoke them to the people in common discourse.

The Church is favored with many excellent productions on the parables. Our design is plain, and we ask the help and blessing of God to carry it to completion. We shall seek to make analyses of ten of the leading parables of our Lord. At first we thought of attempting to show what was contained on each subject in the parables considered together, but on reflection we found that it would produce such a mutilation or severance of them as would greatly mar their beauty and symmetry, and was of doubtful propriety. So on mature consideration we have determined to attempt an analysis of each parable separately, showing the figures employed as to their meaning and design, the chief doctrine presented and the duties prescribed and sins prohibited. Each parable has some history, event, or occupation which constitutes the figure on which it rests. It contains one or more doctrines laid down to the world authoritatively by our Lord. And each one has duties for our observance plainly implied or expressed. We write for the common people, and avoid scholastic terms and doubtful speculations.

Were there no other scriptures than the parables, they would avouch their inspiration from heaven beyond controversy, as they reveal our inward or spiritual nature with the truthful certainty of their being a revelation from God. In them the contrast is strongly drawn between religion and irreligion, virtue and vice, and indeed all the good and evil qualities found in the Church and among men. We have treated each parable in its general specification of these qualities as they are taught therein, believing that our readers will sooner perceive and appreciate the difference between right and wrong conduct shown in this obvious and practical way than in any other mode of presentation.

Webster defines a parable to be "a fable or allegorical relation or representation of something real in life or nature from which a moral is drawn for instruction." Our Watson says a parable is "an allegorical instruction, founded on something real or apparent in nature or history, from which a moral is drawn by comparing it with some other thing in which the people are more immediately concerned." Perhaps the latter definition is more full and satisfactory. It certainly describes well our Lord's parables. Not one of them is founded on any pursuit or history that was unknown or foreign to the people who first heard his parables, or that was of local or temporary use; and now in the nineteenth century after their delivery as we read them we find around us and in every land the same callings and usages of society to which they refer. The natural objects on which the parables rest in the representation are at our door, and the spiritual application is therefore easy, and may be immediately made.

We enter gardens, fields, houses, cities, country-places, private and public homes, amid flowers, fruits, and every variety of innocent enjoyment, so that from the seen we may approach the unseen and believe and live. Our faith will be strengthened and our hand for duty quickened and encouraged until it will be our meat and drink to do the will of God. Let us sit down to a repast from our Lord's parables, following him as our leader, and fearing no evil.

We intend all the profits of this book to go to the Preachers' Aid Society of the Kentucky Conference, Methodist Episcopal Church, South. We regard the most deserving beneficiaries of the Church to-day to be those whom our Discipline designates as "the traveling, supernumerary, superannuated, and worn-out preachers, their wives, widows, and children." Every Conference has them, and God regards them with a tender love. So far as pay is concerned, it was this object alone that made us bold enough to write. Will not every preacher appreciate the motive and help in the sale of the book? S. NOLAND.

CONTENTS.

	PAGE
BISHOP H. H. KAVANAUGH	13
THE SOWER	27
THE TARES	57
THE BARREN FIG-TREE	75
THE DISCOVERIES OF SIN	93
THE PRODIGAL AND THE SELF-RIGHTEOUS SON	102
THE GREAT SUPPER	125
THE GOOD SAMARITAN	143
GOOD WORKS	158
THE PHARISEE AND PUBLICAN	171
THE UNJUST JUDGE	191
THE WISE AND FOOLISH VIRGINS	205
THE RICH MAN AND LAZARUS	216
THE RESURRECTION OF CHRIST	231

SERMONS—PARABLES.

BISHOP H. H. KAVANAUGH.*

"For our light affliction, which is but for a moment, worketh for us a far more exceeding and eternal weight of glory." 2 Cor. iv. 17.

MANY churches and many hearts are opening for memorial services in honor of our beloved and lately deceased Bishop H. H. Kavanaugh. We join to-day in this sad duty with our Church and our country, but our circumstances and our feelings must be different to some extent from all others. If any aim to make a demonstration because he was a good and a great man, and because the Church had elevated him for many years to its most responsible position, we come only to offer hearts of love and minds full of tender memories. He had lived here so long—and in all the years had acted more as the ordinary than as the chief pastor, visiting all the houses and leaving in them his richest Christian benedictions—that we can do no more than meet as a large family of kindred to consider

---

*A memorial sermon preached by Rev. S. Noland at Versailles, Ky., April 6, 1884, by request of the M. E. Church, South, at that place.

our loss and *his* gain by the stroke of death which has removed him from earth to heaven.

Our text is selected this morning because of its own appropriateness, and because our beloved Bishop, in the last attempt that he made to preach, had chosen the same words. Only a few weeks before his decease, he appeared in a pulpit at Ocean Springs anxious once more to proclaim salvation through "the Lamb of God which taketh away the sin of the world," and while unwell announced this text, and after repeating it the third time to the audience was compelled to admit his physical inability to proceed. Physicians and friends attended him, and his voice was no more to be heard in earthly pulpits. For more than sixty years, and probably fifteen thousand times, it had given no uncertain sound in the battle against sin; but now the Master called him away from the conflict. We have thought it would be honoring him to-day to use the same words before the people whom he so long and so dearly loved. We hoped that it would show to some extent that while the ablest ministers fall at their post unable to preach again, the Bible stands open and full of the same precious and comforting texts in all the centuries for other men to use in the Church of God. And it seemed to us that the text commended itself as being entirely appropriate to this occasion, as it presents the view that was often in his mind and heart—earthly afflictions, all light and momentary, ushering the soul at death into "a far more exceeding and eternal weight of glory" in the heavenly state.

In our mind this text in one of its leading features resembles one that we employed on another occasion in this town. Twenty and a half years ago, in a house then belonging to Bishop Kavanaugh, in the presence of many people filling the house and the adjoining grounds, we preached the sermon before the burial of one of the Lord's saints, dear Sister Kavanaugh, from the words, " Precious in the sight of the Lord is the death of his saints." We name a feature in the texts employed of striking similarity and of great importance. It was *death* that was precious in the sight of the Lord, because it was the death of a saint. Now we know that neither the learning nor the philosophy of this world has ever reached that state of perfection where they found any thing *precious in death*. All their study is to avoid it or to bear up under the trial. But the religion of our Heavenly Father lifts us on a higher plane, and shows us a preciousness in this most dreaded enemy. In our text to-day we ascend the same higher plane, which learning and philosophy never reached, and we find that *affliction* is the stepping-stone from earth to heavenly glory. The world finds only unmixed evil in affliction. It is full of bodily pain, and agony of mind, and loss of vital powers, and apprehension of changes worse and worse, until all seems lost to the eye that looks only to mother earth. But in this disorder and distress God opens the eye of faith to see beyond its throes "a far more exceeding and eternal weight of glory."

May we honor the memory of the dear saint whom we have named with the acknowledgment of a personal obligation? On our first visit to this church as its appointed pastor, her quick eye detected in us a delicate hesitancy in entering upon our pastoral work as a stranger, visiting houses where we were unknown and introducing ourself as the preacher in charge. With Christian kindness and thoughtfulness, she offered her services to walk with us to all the Methodist families in town and give us introduction and indorsement. She removed from us a heavy load, and to-day she has our public acknowledgment of her labor of love. Little did we think on the day that she introduced us to the Methodists in Versailles that we should so soon be called to lay her in "the silent city of the dead," and twenty and one-half years afterward to address this large and sympathizing audience on the demise of her honored husband. Surely we may say:

> God moves in a mysterious way
> His wonders to perform;
> He plants his footsteps on the sea
> And rides upon the storm.

We do not propose a *statistical* exhibit on this occasion. The character, life, and example of our Bishop are of more value to us than any number of dates. We have a *good* and a *great* life to present, and the feature most unusual among men is that his goodness exceeds his greatness. Of course we are understood as meaning goodness through grace. In reading biography and individual history of eminent men we have often been pained to find the great events of the life overshadowed by common and unimportant dates. A few days ago the life of Scotland's Dr. Chalmers fell into our hands, and the author was so engrossed with the great deeds which he had performed that he neither told the time of his birth or death. It seemed to us in exquisite taste, and an example so rare that we had seen none like it among uninspired men. Four inspired historians have written the life of Jesus Christ and have given neither the date of his birth, miracles, or death. If these had been given, hero-worship would have followed in all the world and throughout the ages. To-day we seek to remember our friend in the chief qualities of his *character* and *life*.

We begin with some thoughts for the young people of this audience. When a youth, and before he was converted, Bishop Kavanaugh decided to have a *positive* character, and began the formation of the same. God gives us in the morning of life the *power*, not the *right*, to choose between right and wrong. Mark the distinction between power and right as here expressed. No one can be a free agent without the power to choose right or wrong. God made us free agents and placed us here on trial and in a trial state, and the power to do wrong followed this condition. We boast of our liberty of choice, but it is the most fearful responsibility this side of heaven. The right to do wrong could never be granted by a holy God demanding holiness. Hence, as soon as the power to do wrong was laid at the door of our hearts, commands to do right were issued from heaven with all possible motives annexed to insure obedience.

Some young people decide early in life to have a positive character, either to do right or wrong as they may prefer. Perhaps the majority scarcely decide either way, but drift with the chances, and frequently, almost unconsciously to themselves, are found in the way with sinners. One of the most encouraging thoughts that can enter a parent's heart is to see a child from principle take the right side in the issues of life. This may be done before conversion from a perception that the right is always preferable to the wrong, and from a certain nobility of character leading in that way. When such young persons accept religion, they find that it agrees with habits already formed, and begets a lively hope that all evil may be overcome by the grace of God.

But we wish to be particular in explaining to all the young people present the leading features of character formed by our dear friend in his opening life. He was possessed of *firmness* and *kindness* blended in harmony. Some study and watchfulness are necessary to unite these qualities. All his after life showed how admirably they were existing in him. He studied his positions well, he believed he was right, and consequently he seldom changed. But in exercising his episcopal power, he never forgot that the judge is supposed to be on the side of the weak and even of the criminal. A preacher involved in trouble had a host for him if he could enlist Bishop Kavanaugh in his behalf. And these qualities of firmness and kindness went back to the days of his youth, and were qualities of his own choice.

Added to these he had what the world properly calls *honor* and *integrity*. His word was his bond. He never practiced artifice for an hour in his life. He never asked an easy place that others might be sent in his stead to bear hardship. He never rounded a period to hide any part of the truth. He meant all that he said, and no more. These qualities were voluntarily preferred by him to their opposites, and they belonged to him before he was a Christian or a preacher. Having them made religion an easy garment to wear.

Lastly, he *persevered* in any work begun. This

led him to make the most of life, and early to choose one vocation and to follow it through evil and through good report. Life is too short to make changes. Let the young people study well the few positive qualities named.

Prudence and wordly prosperity will approve of the choice made at this period of his life. But one of far greater moment remained to be considered by our beloved Bishop. It was the question of the salvation of his soul by Jesus Christ. He decided to be on the Lord's side, and that gave direction to the whole course of his life. This was his *second* voluntary choice, and was far more important than the first. He sought and found a true conversion, by which he knew for himself that he was a new creature in Christ. Religion with him was a reality a thousand times more than it was a profession. He joined the Church that his name might be registered in her books and at the same time in the Lamb's book of life.

Let us appeal to the good sense of the rising generation while we ask them if each step taken thus far in the life of our honored Bishop was not well and wisely taken. Do you see any one that he could have safely omitted? Suppose his union with the Church had been merely by emotion or excitement, or for credit, or to escape danger, of what real good would such a profession be proof? None at all. We beseech all young people to let the noblest and purest principles of heart and life actuate them when they take upon themselves the vows of the house of God.

Soon the question arose with this young man: "What is my life work? Shall I continue in the printing business, as I have begun?" And then that solemn impression of soul came to him from heaven that every true minister has felt: "Son, go work to-day in my vineyard. Feed my sheep. Feed my lambs. Call sinners to repentance. Go into all the world and preach the gospel to every creature." The call was from God, and he obeyed. This was his *third* voluntary choice, deliberately made. The care of souls was upon him, and he had no time for more than sixty years to do any thing else than preach the unsearchable riches of Christ.

From the first sermon he was popular. He preached with the power of the Holy Ghost sent down from heaven. He had no time for an academic course in the schools, but he studied books and men as he ran, and as he ran he preached. He felt that God had given him a territory greater than the Czar of Russia or the Queen of England possesses. They have metes and bounds, but the world was his parish. He was one of the few men who never sought elevation in the Church of God. Goodness through grace was in his heart, and the care of all the churches was laid upon him by his brethren. He was one of the few men who remained unchanged by elevation, the only effect being to increase his sense of responsibility and his desire to do good. We knew him for more than forty years, and heard him preach in the station, in the district, in the episcopal office, in the mountains and in the city, and at all times and in all places the message, the manner, and the result were the same.

What did he preach in all the years of his useful life?

He studied a few books thoroughly. The Bible was the book by which he tried all others. In doctrine he was an Arminian Methodist; and he held the tenets of his Church with unwavering fidelity. He studied Wesley, Watson, and Fletcher, comparing them with the Scriptures, and reading them with a view to find truth and not error. He did not expect to get beyond them in knowledge. They were orthodox and scriptural, and he was satisfied with these qualities. He studied Watson's Institutes for more than sixty years. It would be difficult for any intelligent man to doubt the truthfulness of the Scriptures if he read carefully the first volume of this work without prejudice. It has been said that Gov. Owsley, before and after he had retired from the Appellate Bench, read Blackstone every year. All lawyers will understand the significance of this remark.

So Bishop Kavanaugh studied Watson; so our preachers should study him at this day. They should sit at his feet, and not present the ridiculous appearance of trying to lead him. Watson was called of God to give a clear exposition of the Scriptures, and to draw the line of truth half way between Antinomianism and Pelagianism.

Every Bible student knows that no finite mind can see all its truths in one view. There must be leading divisions for study, faith, and duty. So Bishop Kavanaugh studied the Bible, and found it contained the following general truths, which he preached throughout his ministry.

He learned from the Scriptures that there was one living and true God, and in the Godhead there were three Persons—Father, Son, and Holy Ghost, a trinity in unity. The Scriptures taught him that Jesus Christ was divine and human, the latter nature being voluntarily taken by him for the redemption of our race. In the best possible faith he found from the word of God that Christ, by his death, made atonement for the sins of the whole world, so that, while infants are born with a morally corrupt nature, they and all others dying before actual sins of their own are committed are saved in heaven. He held from the Scriptures that the Holy Spirit personally and actually convicts men of sin, gives them repentance and faith, regenerates and sanctifies them, and continues to bear witness in believers as long as they are faithful. While the Saviour and the Holy Spirit both influence men through the word and by other means, he found that both had direct and personal access to the heart and life of all who believe. By the fall, he found that man had lost the image and likeness of God in which he was created, and had become totally depraved in his whole moral and spiritual nature. He found that man can only return to the favor of God through his Son by faith in his righteousness. After the soul was regenerated, he learned through the Scriptures that there was only a possibility, but a very plain possibility, that the Christian might depart from God and lose salvation. He ascertained that good works in the religious life were indispensable, as God would judge all men by the deeds done in the body; but there was to be no merit ascribed to good works as the procuring cause of salvation. After death, he found that the Scriptures taught that there was an actual eternal heaven for the righteous and an actual eternal hell for the wicked. These were the chief doctrines which he believed and preached with wonderful power for more than sixty years.

Bishop Kavanaugh was welcomed by every Conference as its presiding officer. His genial nature made all love him as a father. His long association with men had given him a wonderful insight into their nature and character. No man was a better judge than he of the right man for the right place. The preachers were safer in his hands than they were in their own, as he knew better than they their capacity and place. Woe to the man whose vanity or forwardness came before the keen wit of Bishop Kavanaugh! He not only fell, but he *knew* that he had fallen.

We close with naming his extraordinary faith. First, he had unwavering faith in the *Church* and its success. He always saw it as the Church of God. He knew its strength was from heaven and not from earth. Divisions and declensions were only temporary hinderances in his mind. The lecture of an infidel was so ineffectual, in his mind, to disturb Christianity that it was beneath his notice. In each believer he realized that his body was the temple of the Holy Ghost. In each society of believers he held that two could put ten thousand of the wicked to flight. This cheerful and encouraging view of the Church made him love all denominations. Without compromising any truth, he offered his hand and heart in true fraternity to all who claimed Jesus as their Lord. Second, he had daily, personal, abiding, and conscious *faith in Christ*. He walked with Jesus in spirit as truly as if he had traveled with him bodily in Galilee or Jerusalem. So he lived, and so he died. "A far more exceeding and eternal weight of glory" is his reward. Choose ye his God, and discard Baal.

We have said but little to-day about death. To those who are scarcely saved, death seems an immense and fearful crossing from time to eternity; but our beloved Bishop, with all the true elect of God, must be seen in their lives, and to them bodily death is only a single step and the narrowest passway from earth to the paradise of God. Hence all descriptions of death on this occasion would be wide of our aim and unnecessary in speaking of one who could exclaim, "O death, where is thy sting? O grave where is thy victory?" It has been all life for more than sixty years with our brother, and death was a line so small between time and eternity as to be almost invisible, while light and life continue in all the ages to come. Be ye also ready.

OUR LORD'S PARABLES.

The Sower.

"Behold, there went out a sower to sow; and it came to pass, as he sowed, some fell by the way-side, and the fowls of the air came and devoured it up. And some fell on stony ground, where it had not much earth; and immediately it sprung up, because it had no depth of earth; but when the sun was up, it was scorched; and because it had no root, it withered away. And some fell among thorns, and the thorns grew up, and choked it, and it yielded no fruit. And other fell on good ground, and did yield fruit that sprung up and increased, and brought forth, some thirty, and some sixty, and some a hundred." Mark iv. 3-8.

THE parable of the sower is among the first of all our Lord's parables. It evidently made a deep impression when it was spoken, as three of the sacred writers give it a place in their Gospel. Founded on agricultural life, it is adapted to all lands and times, as perhaps a majority of all who read it will be employed in tilling the ground. As city, town, and country, all depend upon the cultivated field for bodily sustenance, this parable is eminently proper as showing, in the very beginning of our

Saviour's ministry, the nature of his gospel in giving spiritual light and life to all men.

Matthew and Mark record this parable in exactly six verses each, while Luke, whose style is always perspicuous, employs only four verses. As a proof that this was not by concert of action between them, we have but to state to the reader that the original manuscript of the Gospels was not divided into verses and chapters, but this division is a work of later date. As an unusual number of figures appear in the recital—sower, seed, ground, way-side, thorny ground, good ground, thirty, sixty, and a hundred fold of grain, and other circumstances—the belief is strong that the parable made a deep impression on their minds from the lucid and brief statement of all its terms by three writers, in nearly the same number of words.

We believe that the products of the field earned by the sweat of the brow were intended before all other work to be the employment of the large majority of mankind after the fall. The country is large and the town small in the comparison. Cowper wrote, "God made the country and man made the town." Vast acres are spread over all the land adapted to every variety of growth known to man. All the industries are studied by men with great labor of invention and experiment, but God makes the soil and the seed, and gives the rain and the sunshine, and the right temperature, and man only applies his gifts, and the earth brings forth seed-time and harvest. How many young men miss the noblest calling of life when they refuse to cultivate the field!

In this parable *every thing is good* until disturbed by a foreign element—a good sower, good seed, good ground, good year, good harvest. All the failures recorded are left without excuse, as every help was furnished to avoid them.

Let us consider separately the figures employed.

The sower is first named. Mark says, "There went out a sower to sow." Matthew says, "Behold a sower went forth to sow." Luke says, "A sower went out to sow his seed." Each begins the parable with the sower and his specific work. We know that the chief sower is the Son of God, from the fact that the seed sown is the word of God, and he is the author and giver of that word. We also know that his ministers and other servants, under him and by his appointment, are sowers of the word of life. We are thankful that the parable and our work together begin with Jesus Christ. All true religion begins with God, and every moment of its continuance depends on his grace. The Bible began with God: "In the beginning God created the heaven and the earth." The gospel begins with God and his Son: "In the beginning was the Word, and the Word was with God, and the Word was God." Let us begin aright. "For other foundation can no man lay than that is laid, which is Christ Jesus."

Behold the activity of Jesus as the Chief Sower! He went forth to sow the seed of truth. Paul passed two years in his own hired house preaching the gospel, and this is the longest pastorate known in the New Testament. The twelve apostles, the seventy, and all the ministers in the days of our Lord, were heeding a command from heaven which said, "Go ye into all the world and preach the gospel to every creature." The Czar of all the Russias has a limited territory; the minister of Christ alone can say, "The world is my parish." The pious Montgomery has taught us to sing:

> Sow in the morn thy seed,
>   At eve hold not thy hand;
> To doubt and fear give thou no heed—
>   Broadcast it o'er the land.
>
> Beside all waters sow,
>   The highway furrows stock,
> Drop it where thorns and thistles grow,
>   Scatter it on the rock.

Our Chief Sower went about doing good. City, town, and country were all visited on his missions of mercy. He was our Chief Itinerant. In a ministry of only three years' continuance he preached all over Palestine, receiving no salary, working a miracle to pay a poll-tax, and saying of himself, "The foxes have holes, and the birds of the air have nests, but the Son of man hath not where to lay his head." His example of constant labor is our model. He was ever instant in season and out of season.

Consider a moment the unreasonableness of our complaints. We believe that twenty years is more than the average period of effective work with our ministers as a body. Four years is the legal limitation of time in one work. A preacher may stay one-fifth of his time in a single charge. With a jurisdiction that extends to all the world, he contents himself as doing his whole duty by preaching four years to two hundred people on the Sabbath-day, and those the same people all the time. Possibly he is dissatisfied with the law of the Church when he is required to go to another field of labor at the end of four years. He has gifts that would be effective in reaching some hearts in all places, but he expends his strength on the same people year after year. He voluntarily accepted the itinerant field as his life-work, and yet locality seems to him the ecstasy of bliss. Instead of sowing the whole field, as the Master did, he has only sowed as much ground as his own lot in the cemetery.

The seed is the word of God. When Satan tempted Jesus, our Lord used only the word of God, repelling every temptation with an apt quotation after the words, "It is written." Consider a moment the word of God—the Bible. The book as it now stands was fifteen hundred years in preparation. We doubt whether any book of man can number more than one hundred years from its commencement to its completion. More than two thousand years had elapsed before any portion of the word of God was given, so that mankind might be able to disprove its claims if they were false from the time of writing the first page. Some forty authors composed the Holy Scriptures, all scripture being given by inspiration of God. Every variety of scholarship and talent is employed, the writers living centuries apart, and the themes above the compass of uninspired men. God, eternity, heaven, hell, redemption, sin, holiness, duty, angels, and devils, are a few of the subjects largely treated in this wonderful volume. No amount of scientific discovery or philosophic speculation ever explained these grand subjects to mankind. Here, under the claim of inspiration from heaven, some forty authors, without the least confederation or consultation with one another, bring them to the observation and faith of men as plainly as if they were only the rudimentary principles of knowledge on the subjects named. In all the book nothing wrong is ever tolerated, and all that is right is taught and commanded. Every step of public and private life may be safely taken by the light of this book. Is it not the truth from heaven?

The field of the parable is the world, and the sower sowed the seed over the whole field. Here we find the first equality among men. Not a line of the Bible was written exclusively for royal eyes, and not a line that the peasant may not read, believe, and obey. God is no respecter of persons, but mankind are selfish, and have never learned to regard the poor as favorably as the rich and to honor the humble as truly as the proud and great of the earth. The most striking difference between the Christian system and every other is its equality of consideration for all conditions of life.

The sower sowed the whole field. John said, "The whole world lieth in wickedness." Jesus taught us that "God so loved the world that he gave his only-begotten Son, that whosoever believeth in him might not perish, but have everlasting life." But with all this equal love of God for all nations and all times, and his imperative command to sow the good seed in all the world by various agencies duly appointed and commissioned, what painful sight do we behold! After furnishing the Church seed, which, if planted and cultivated, would produce at the minimum estimate thirty-fold increase, so as to enlarge the capacity to produce more, we find in the nineteenth century only a small part of the globe on which the good seed has been sown. The largest part of its area is held in chains by idolatry, superstition, and the devil. Civilization and peace among all men are held back by this want of imitation of our Chief Sower, and ignorance, war, and all manner of crime run riot over the earth. How long, O Lord, how long, before all Christians shall coöperate and put forth all their strength to go or send the good seed into every nook and cranny of this sinful world?

The last figure is the good result. Thirty, sixty, and a hundred fold is a wonderful increase in any department of life. But this is simply the power of truth over error, and of righteousness over ungodliness. The wicked often suppose that they have accomplished vastly more than the righteous because their flourish of trumpets has been heard, and the cry, "Great is Diana of the Ephesians!" has been repeated from age to age and from nation to nation. Still the permanent result is no more than firing blank cartridges in a fierce battle. The wicked shall not live out half their days, and their plans are not better or more secure than their life. The psalmist teaches us in the first Psalm that even their way shall perish while they are yet alive. There is no agreed concert of action between the wicked, no faith in their leadership, no monuments of charity for the suffering to endear the world to them, and all their pleasures, fashions, and pursuits changing from youth to manhood and from manhood to old age.

In opposition to the wicked, the righteous know that all truth is immortal. They know that Jesus is the truth, the way, and the life. They realize that the blessing of truth to themselves would be an equal blessing if the same truth should be carried to the ends of the earth. The spires of their

THE SOWER. 35

churches, orphanages, and colleges, which point toward heaven in the name of the crucified One, are equally needed in China, Japan, the isles of the ocean, and all the places of the earth inhabited by man. The least gain expected is thirty-fold. Every prayer offered to the Lord of hosts by his children in the words "Thy kingdom come" expects this amount of increase, or more. No Christian believes that the word of the Lord shall return void from any place at any time. We now have notable instances in the heathen world, occurring almost every month, where men of superior mind and large influence, without examining the abundant proofs miracles and prophecy afford, believe our religion is true, and yield their hearts and lives to the service of Christ, from the beautiful lessons of virtue and love taught in his word. The seed therefore commends itself as being good by its own appearance and results.

The doctrine taught in this parable is the one above all others that we rejoice to know the Lord stated plainly in the beginning of his parables. In the atonement of Christ propitiation is made for the sins of the whole world, and in his crucifixion he tasted death for every man. The good sower sowed the good seed over the whole field, which is the world. Whosoever will may take the water of life freely, and may eat and live. The way-side, the rocky ground, and the thorny ground received the best seed from the kind hands that scattered it in all places in unsparing measure and with unceasing care.

That our blessed Lord in good faith died for all men is now more generally believed than it was one hundred years ago or more, when Methodism took its rise in England. The writings of Fletcher, Wesley, Watson, Benson, and Clarke silenced Calvinism forever as to its grand error of election and reprobation. From the belief in the decree of God held by Calvin, which he admitted was a horrible decree, by which a certain number of adults and infants were supposed to be consigned to everlasting wrath from eternity, to its most modified form as taught by Baxter and others, where a general atonement is admitted and a special application in the same moment held, by which only the elect can believe on Christ, there is nothing in the schemes consistent with reason or taught in Scripture. No good purpose of morals is served by this error, nor is there a ray of comfort to any soul, as all are obliged to pass their pilgrimage uncertain whether they are elect or reprobate. It would be a distressing thought that in every family of three the probability would be that at least one was reprobate, and possibly that one the infant at its mother's breast.

This error originated in the truth that God is sovereign and does the work of our salvation, and that no saving righteousness attaches to any of our works of obedience. So we see that error may spring from truth. Both these views are held as firmly by Wesleyan Arminians as by any form of Calvinism, and with reason and Scripture to support them. It is wholly unnecessary to assert an eternal purpose and decree of God to make him a Sovereign, because without these he is a Sovereign in consequence of being our Creator, King, and Redeemer. It is wholly unnecessary to assert the passivity of man in every religious act to avoid the claim of merit on his part for his acts of obedience, because the blood of Christ and his substitution to the law of God in our stead will as effectually silence every whisper of merit.

We believe that the greatest difficulty in freeing the mind from this Calvinistic error arises from the supposition that the foreknowledge of God necessarily implies that he has decreed all things to the extent of that knowledge. As plainly illogical as this view is, still it is the stumbling-block in many minds. To us it seems strange that any one should suppose that the knowledge of a thing is necessarily the cause of the thing known. The existence of the things known, as a general rule, is prior to the knowledge of them, and of all such things the knowledge cannot be the cause. And where the things known are to take place in the future, it is evident that the knowledge is distinct from the event, as the event cannot exist until the future time arrives. Still we are met with the question, "If God foreknows all things, will they not come to pass just as he foreknew them?" We answer: "Yes; but this is no proof that God decreed that they should come to pass." From the unlimited perfections of God, he must foreknow all things. Known unto God are all his works from the beginning of the world. But our own consciousness assures us that the knowledge of God is no constraint upon our will. We may choose or reject, and we voluntarily do these things every day of our lives. His knowledge no more controls our will than his power keeps our arm from moving. God is omnipotent—by which we mean that he is all-powerful; and yet we are very sure that we have some power. The Lord has not kept in his own hand a monopoly of power because he has all power; nor has he kept a monopoly of knowledge because he has all wisdom. His attributes never interfere with the free use of our ability. He is a helping and not a hindering God.

It would be impossible to assign a satisfactory reason for a limited atonement. The only reason that has even a show of plausibility is that God may do as he will with his own. But this statement must be received so as to harmonize all his attributes. We are not to suppose that because God is omnipotent he could therefore justly send the holy angels of heaven to hell. The very thought is shocking and monstrous. Neither may we suppose that God could bring a descendant of Adam into the world without his consent, with the corruption of moral nature that would attach to him, and then by an irreversible decree, written in the past eternity, doom this person to an eternal hell for rejecting Christ, when the same decree had made it impossible for him to accept Christ.

Our Lord affirmed that he had not come to call the righteous, but sinners, to repentance. According to the error that we are opposing, if it had been true he would have said: "I am not come to call sinners, but the elect, to a hope which they cannot lose, either in this world or the world to come." But he strangely reverses it, and calls those to repentance whom the decree supposes cannot be saved. Paul says that Jesus came into the world to save sinners; the error says that he came to save the elect. Ezekiel says that "God has no pleasure in the death of him that dieth;" but the error says that this death was ordered from eternity, and that God has pleasure only in those who were decreed to eternal life. Just at the close of the Scriptures it is said that "whosoever will may take the water of life freely;" but the error has decided that all the reprobate cannot have any will under God's decree to take the water of life.

When our Lord was dying, he prayed for his murderers: "Father, forgive them, for they know not what they do." Can any one believe that these murderers were a body of the elect who might receive our Lord's prayers to their spiritual profit? Can any one believe that if they had been reprobated from all eternity Jesus would have prayed to his Father for their forgiveness, when he knew that their forgiveness was an impossibility? The truth is, they were all sinners for whom Christ was dying, and in their hearing, with the desire that some of them might turn and live, he made the prayer. At least one poor wretch at his side did turn and live, and on that day entered paradise.

The duty taught in this parable is continuance in well-doing and avoiding the enemies of our souls who beset us from within and without.

From the day that the seed was sown until the day that the harvest was gathered, there was never an hour when it could stop growing and live. Without soil, sunshine, rain, and culture, it would soon die. It could only strengthen and mature by a continuance of growth. Each one of its enemies, left alone, would insure its death. If the seed fell on the way-side and remained there unprotected, the birds of the air soon devoured it up. If we remain out of the Church and with sinners, our ruin is soon complete. If an unremoved rock should be beneath and near the seed, a shallow soil would not long protect the young growth, but the heat of the sun would presently stop its growth and destroy its life. If our religion begins with excitement and emotion that cannot last long, taunts and opposition will destroy our religious life as soon as the first days are past. If thorns are allowed to grow where the seed is growing, their roots and their trunk, and their branches and their shade, will soon produce death. So if all worldly cares and pleasures are allowed a place in our hearts with the good seed, soon or late they will be our master and we shall fall from grace. Keeping these suggestions in mind, let us consider the varieties of soil and result in detail.

The way-side hearer is first named. "And it came to pass, as he sowed, some fell by the way-side, and the fowls of the air came and devoured it up." "These are they by the way-side, where the word is sown; but when they have heard, Satan cometh immediately, and taketh away the word that was sown in their hearts." Strictly, a way-side is the border of a path or road, but here it is the entire line of travel. It was made over the field after the sower had prepared that part of the ground for the reception of the seed. The hearts of the young are so prepared by divine grace that all the good seed of the word of God would produce fruit, if it were not for the fact that a way-side is made in them before the time for sowing the precious seed of divine truth. A well-remembered part of our boyhood history will illustrate how a way-side is made. Our father was a school-teacher, and a new school-house was built for his occupancy, but to reach it all the scholars had to pass through a dense wood nearly a mile, and where no path or road had ever been made. To keep the children from missing the way, our father blazed the trees with an ax. This led each child to walk in the same place. In a short time a pathway became perceptible, which became harder and easier seen as it was more and more used; and it was observed that as soon as this way-side was distinguishable the blazed trees were forgotten. So when a way-side of sinful thoughts or actions is once formed in the heart, only to a small extent, the teachings of parents, ministers, and others are set aside and begin to fade from the memory.

The way-side hearers are those who have ears to hear and hear not. They take no heed how they hear. Gallio was a way-side hearer who cared for none of those things which were spoken. Ephraim was a way-side hearer who became joined to his idols until the Lord said, "Let him alone." Our Lord had some way-side hearers who made light of all his teachings. In the parable of the Great Supper there were three classes of way-side hearers who avoided the invitation to the feast when they began with one consent to make excuse. All atheists, infidels, and deists are way-side hearers, being evil classes of men who ignore the government of God from different stand-points, but in whose hearts the good seed finds no lodgment for a single hour or day. The way-side hearers are those who enter the church and leave at the close of the service without receiving any impression for good, and possibly without being able to remember the text, hymns, prayers, or any part of the sermon.

On the heart of a way-side hearer the seed falls without entering to any extent. And then immediately the birds of the air with their keen eyes in the figure, but Satan in reality, snatch the seed and devour it up. Even on this hard way-side, if the seed remain until the warm and gentle rains fall, representing the grace and Spirit of God, they might grow and produce fruit. Hence Satan does his evil work immediately. In his ranks such a thing as procrastination is unknown. The unsuspecting victim is not left time to think, feel, reason, or act, but instantly, and with the clear vision of a bird searching for seed, he takes away every good impression.

The same field may have various way-sides. One may run across the field for the convenience of one party, another may run across the corners of the field, and another along the line of one or more of the sides of the field. The grumbler may have one way-side, the swearer another, the drunkard a third, the lover of pleasure one of a kind different from the rest, and the unbeliever and practical sinner a way-side adapted to their vicious tastes. Notice that a way-side occupies the least ground of any part of the field, and yet it is traveled more than all the rest. Wickedness follows on the heels of wickedness, the heart of one hardening the heart of another, until the ungodly stand in a solid column of opposition to the laws of Heaven.

Evidently the way-side hearers give Satan far less trouble in effecting their ruin than either of the other classes. They are already sold under sin. As to many of them, their sins are gone to judgment beforehand. They have hardened their hearts and stiffened their necks against all divine teaching and influence, and their consciences are seared as with a hot iron. A dream that we read years ago will illustrate the proceedings of Satan with them. The writer dreamed that he had taken his seat at the side of a distinguished preacher, to hear him preach for the first time. The hearer sat facing the audience, and the preacher's subject was the sower. While he was depicting the way-side hearers, a man in the audience, dressed in black and of strange appearance, began gathering up the seed that was falling on the crowd. It soon appeared that he had devoured up all the seed, and then the dreamer discovered it was the devil. The next day, riding along the road and thinking of the strange occurrence at the meeting, he passed a saloon where men were drinking, swearing, and fighting, and he dreamed he entered, with the expectation that he would find the man in black as he had seen him the day before. To his surprise, after the most careful search, he was not found. Pursuing his journey, unexpectedly, he came across the man in black lying by the road-side asleep. Awaking him, he said: "If you will go back to the saloon you can find a number of men whom you can easily influence to act with you in evil." The devil replied: "You do not understand my mission. Those men in the saloon are graduates of mine, and need no training. I am resting to-day, as a camp-meeting will begin to-morrow in this neighborhood, and if you attend there you will see the character of my work displayed to advantage in many ways."

Next come the stony ground hearers. "And some fell on stony ground, where it had not much earth, and immediately it sprung up, because it had no depth of earth; but when the sun was up, it was scorched; and because it had no root, it withered away." "And these are they likewise which are sown on stony ground; who, when they have heard the word, immediately receive it with gladness; and have no root in themselves, and so endure but for a time; afterward, when affliction or persecution ariseth for the word's sake, immediately they are offended."

The advantage of this class of hearers over the way-side hearers is only apparent and temporary. It is only apparent because the hidden rock just beneath the surface is as certain, and probably more certain, to destroy the fruit than the way-side ground, as that could be improved by culture and softened by the rain. Often it is true that the worst sinners become the best Christians if they can be persuaded to repent, while those who from mere excitement profess religion soonest forsake and neglect the altars of the Church. The prodigal son, for a time, was much farther gone in wickedness than his elder brother, but when he came to himself his repentance and faith had more genuine proofs than the other. He who said, "I go not," and afterward repented and went, was commended beyond the man who said at once, "I go, sir," and went not.

The class of hearers here specified act more from impulse and excitement than from conviction and reason. They will profess religion under any doctrines in any Church, if the community attending that Church is moved with religious fervor. They will not profess religion alone, nor join the Church alone, but at some opportune moment, when certain persons are at the altar of prayer, or have offered themselves as members, they will do the same thing; or if a certain minister has preached, or certain hymns or songs are sung which are known to be their favorites, they will act immediately. So it is evident that no heart-principle, or repentance toward God, or faith in Christ, have influenced their conduct, but the surrounding circumstances in which they happen to be placed have impelled the step they have taken. There is no depth of earth and no root in themselves, and therefore under the rays of the sun, intended to give life to all who can bear them, they perish from excess of heat. Even the sun becomes a savor of death unto death.

Two things hasten the ruin of all stony ground hearers—affliction and persecution. Their religion is adapted only to a healthy body and mind, and the encouragement of friends. Satan knows well enough that affliction and persecution will always appear as trials in every religious professor's life, the faithful enduring to the end, the unstable falling before their power. They are certain tests of character which separate the precious from the vile. Afflictions are not so likely to succeed when alone in causing him who has put his hand to the plow to look back, hence persecutions are added to them to complete the trial. The afflictions and persecutions named are for the word's sake, or on account of the profession of religion made, and for no other cause or of any other kind. It may be that the persecution is in the mild form of a laugh or a sneer from the thoughtless, or it may be the indignation of a parent toward a child, or the censure of a community toward one who following his own convictions of right and duty has left its ranks; but in whatever form it comes, it is the most dangerous trial of the religious life.

Be it observed that the grace of God implanted in any soul has such power that, although formed only in stony ground, it cannot be dislodged merely by the birds of the air devouring it, but the combined powers of affliction and persecution are necessary, aided by the father of lies, to turn the soul back to the beggarly elements of the world. This thought gives abundance of encouragement to every Christian to fight the good fight of faith and endure to the end. Let it not be supposed that the chances, humanly speaking, are barely equal that a Christian will be saved or lost. The probability is as a hundred to one that by the grace of God, the influence of the Church, and his own conscious experience of pardoned sins and the new life, he will overcome the world. "Let him that thinketh he standeth take heed lest he fall," and let him be "persuaded at the same time that neither life, nor death, nor principalities, nor powers, nor things present, nor things to come, nor any other creature, shall be able to separate him from the love of God which is in Christ Jesus our Lord."

We now reach the thorny ground hearers, where the responsibility is vastly increased, from the fact that no fault is found with the seed falling on a hard way-side, nor on ground where rocks unseen are near the surface, but a class of surroundings which might be extirpated or avoided become their ruin. "And some fell among thorns, and the thorns grew up and choked it, and it yielded no fruit." "And these are they which are sown among thorns;

such as hear the word, and the cares of this world, and the deceitfulness of riches, and the lusts of other things entering in, choke the word, and it becometh unfruitful." The most despisable and ignominious fate is to be choked to death. Morally it is a fearful state of the heart to have all its virtue and finer spiritual sensibility destroyed, by the use and love of carnal and physical objects taken so near the heart as to stop its pulsations and choke it to inaction and loss of life.

As the ground improves Satan finds more influences are necessary to be brought on the field to insure the destruction of the soul. On the way-side ground the keen eyes of the birds succeeded in finding and destroying the seed; on the stony ground it was necessary to have affliction and persecution to reach the end; while on the thorny ground the cares of the world, the deceitfulness of riches, and the lusts of other things are all essential to steal the heart away from the love of God. But Satan will provide as many influences as are necessary to effect the ruin of the soul in every heart where that ruin is not prevented by the removal of all noxious things and the bestowment of all heavenly supplies.

The cares of the world, the deceitfulness of riches, and the lusts of other things embrace all sinful desires and pursuits. And no wonder that all these should be necessary to win souls away from the love of so good a thing as pure and undefiled religion.

If the cares of the world fail to disturb the quietude of the believer in Jesus, then the devil adds to them the deceitfulness of riches; and if both fail, then he brings in promiscuously the lusts of other things, even of all things that please the eye, the ear, the tongue, the emotions, and the heart. When the whole round of worldly appliances are exhausted and the believer maintains his integrity, then is it demonstrated that he is in good ground, producing fruit. But every one will be tried in all these ways, and will find that it is through much tribulation that he must enter into the kingdom of heaven.

The cares of the world are increased by the gratification of all our desires. We ask and receive of a worldly kind, and our very success has increased our trouble and danger. Every desire belonging to earth should be limited by the petition, "Not my will but thine be done." As cares multiply and increase with every change, and especially with all accumulation, we cannot be judges of the quantity of things of the earth that we should have intrusted to us.

The deceitfulness of riches is proverbial, viewed in every light. The deceit begins with a denial on the part of almost every man that he is rich. Paradoxical as it may appear, many men imagine a keen sense of added poverty with added wealth. As an abiding possession nothing is more deceitful than riches. Literally they take to themselves wings and fly away. Thieves break through and steal, moth corrupts, stocks lose their value, mortgages are technically defective, the law's delays hold back the price, investments are made on a mistaken judgment of the outcome, profits are counted while losses and expenses are overlooked, and when the whole estate is vested in land and the title secured beyond controversy, the soil on the surface of the ground disappears year by year until the possessor is left in poverty. How often the expectation of heirs as to riches becomes a failure! The change of trades and pursuits to make more gain is as unreliable as the wind that blows in the morning from the east, and in the evening from the west or south. "Go to now, ye that say, To-day or to-morrow we will go into such a city, and continue there a year, and buy and sell and get gain, whereas ye know not what shall be on the morrow."

"The lusts of other things" includes all doubtful and sinful pleasures. It is only by abstaining from all appearance of evil that we shall overcome this last gilded bait of Satan. All the kingdoms of the world and the glory of them are here displayed and offered; and as these were Satan's last inducement to our Saviour in the temptation, so will he make them the last offer to us. Happy is the man that endureth temptation. The man who walks by the rule that he will in any thing violate the law of the Church in having the desires of his heart gratified will undoubtedly fall. There is no time to indulge supposed small sins or proximity to acknowledged danger. "Escape for thy life, and tarry not in all the plain." The very air stinks with the lusts of other things. "But thou, O man of God, flee these things; flee also youthful lusts."

We close with the good ground hearers. Every principle that can produce or continues involuntarily is destroyed. Sower, seed, culture, sunshine, rains, growth, and ripening, are all good. As there were three varieties of hearers whose life was a failure, so in those who succeed and reach heaven there are in this life three varieties or degrees of success—thirty, sixty, and a hundred fold. The seed and the soil are alike good, and even perfect; but the capacity and industry of some in improving their gifts are greater than others. "And other fell on good ground, and did yield fruit that sprung up and increased, and brought forth, some thirty, and some sixty, and some a hundred." "And these are they which are sown on good ground; such as hear the word, and receive it, and bring forth fruit, some thirty-fold, some sixty, and some a hundred."

On the question of acreage alone, no doubt the good ground outnumbered the way-side, the rocky ground, and the thickets of thorns, as ten or more outnumber one. The infants who are all saved when they die in infancy will probably number more than all lost sinners. The Revelation gives the number of the redeemed who have their Father's name written in their foreheads as being a hundred, forty, and four thousand—a definite for a large and indefinite number. The saved are the rule, the lost the exception.

And not only do the good ground hearers outnumber the other classes in acreage, but also in influence. Observe that the least influence of the humblest and most obscure Christian was thirty-fold, its first gain a double increase, and the last gain a hundred-fold—stated as the maximum of numbers indicating all attainable excellence. General wickedness obtains in all the world, but specific acts as a rule have no record to follow them, and they die and are soon forgotten. The way-side hearers had no influence at all, the stony ground hearers soon died, and the thorny ground hearers exerted no influence, but were choked to death by their evil associations. The psalmist taught us that the very way of the ungodly shall perish; his hopes and pursuits all have to be changed repeatedly before he dies. Youth has one class of pleasures, manhood another, and age a third, each and all of them ephemeral and unsatisfying in their nature; and no more pitiable object can be conceived than an old sinner who is living with only a few days left and without God in the world, even his former friends and enjoyments having left him all alone to die and be forgotten. Not so the righteous. Every religious principle is as fresh and green in old age as it was in youth. It is born of immortality, and can neither fade nor die. A cup of cold water given to a disciple in the name of our Lord shall not lose its reward nor be forgotten. The way-side that destroyed others was only a safe road for the feet of those who went into the field to gather the fruit of the good; the sun that scorched the stony ground hearers was essential aid to the rains, the soil, and the cultivation that so increased the fruits of the good ground; and even the thorns were so used by the righteous as forming a temporary shade for the laborers, employing the world and riches and the various pursuits of the world as necessary possessions of the body and mind in the present pilgrimage, but all subordinate to the heavenly Canaan.

What were the chief items of perfection that so distinguished the good ground hearers, producing such an abundant harvest as to equal the seven years of Egyptian plenty in the days of Joseph? To get rid of sin, all true Christians have voluntarily emptied themselves of self-righteousness. They have not attempted to cure death with a disease, for they know that without the grace of God they are dead in trespasses and sins, and that their own righteousness is as filthy rags that will generate disease in the body unless removed. The first religious feeling is one of shame, producing repentance toward God, and then for the first time in the life of that penitent soul there is joy in heaven, in the presence of the angels of God at the sight of that repentance. A deep consciousness of want at once impels such a sinner away from his own works, both as to their performance and merit, and to lay hold on Christ Jesus through faith as the only one who is mighty and able to save. All the time, just as the sun and the light, and the atmosphere and the rains, and the soil and the assiduous culture, have helped the good seed first to die, and then to live, and then to grow, and then to produce fruit, so the Holy Spirit in conviction, in repentance, in faith, in regeneration, and in growth in grace, has strengthened and sanctified the trusting soul until it passes from death unto life and is made every whit whole.

It is high time to carry the good seed of the kingdom into all the world. The sower intended it for the whole field, but think how many million acres to-day have never received so much as one seed into their bosom! "Go or send," is the motto. This is the true Christian tocsin of war against ungodliness, the Christian flag of "peace on earth, good-will toward men." The whole world lieth in wickedness, and more than half of it in palpable heathen darkness that can be seen and felt. "Come over into Macedonia and help us!" is a cry that has not ceased for nearly twenty centuries. Shall the world continue a barren way-side, a fruitless stony ground, and a choked growth of thorns, while we have the good seed of the kingdom, withholding it from general use? Let us go forth and sow the field. Let this centennial year produce abundant fruit.

The Tares.

"The kingdom of heaven is likened unto a man which sowed good seed in his field; but while men slept, his enemy came and sowed tares among the wheat, and went his way. But when the blade was sprung up, and brought forth fruit, then appeared the tares also. So the servants of the householder came and said unto him, Sir, didst not thou sow good seed in thy field? From whence then hath it tares? He said unto them, An enemy hath done this. The servants said unto him, Wilt thou then that we go and gather them up? But he said, Nay; lest while ye gather up the tares, ye root up also the wheat with them. Let both grow together until the harvest; and in the time of the harvest I will say to the reapers, Gather ye together first the tares, and bind them in bundles to burn them; but gather the wheat into my barn." Matt. xiii. 24–30.

MATTHEW alone records the parable of the tares. Very wisely he places it just after the parable of the sower, as it is its counterpart. Its figures begin precisely as those of the sower, but they soon change, and bring to light other agencies and powers not developed in that parable. In both parables Christ explained all the figures and terms used, because he was asked to do so by his disciples. It is a notable instance of receiving very important information by soliciting the knowledge. Aware of their ignorance, the disciples sought clearer light from the wisdom of their Lord, and thereby gained for themselves and all men a lucid exposition of words which, without it, would have left the best men in serious doubts, and filled the Church with controversy. We are taught in this example that we may always ask the Master, who will open our eyes to see the truth, and we shall certainly receive if we ask humbly and in faith.

Notice that in this parable, as in the former, the sower of the good seed is the Son of man. Here he tells us the figure applies to himself. There we gained the knowledge of the fact because the seed was the word of God, and the Son of God gave us his word. In this parable, as in the other, the field is the world; so we may expect in the same sower and on the same ground the same activity, the same gracious providence, the same equal love, and the same happy results; and we would be surprised if enemies and opposition did not abound as in the other description. In this expectation we will not be disappointed, for we shall find, even in the figure employed, that here a change begins from the *word* to *living persons;* and to effect the ruin of the latter, the machinations of wickedness are brought to light in all their arts of deception, and in all their power of injury.

While the sower and the field are the same in both parables, the seed sown is different; and here

The Tares.

a marked departure begins. In the former parable the seed was the *word of God;* in this it is the *children of the kingdom.* With what inimitable tenderness of expression does our Lord here speak of his followers as children of the kingdom! They are soon to be exposed to severe tests and dangerous associations; and like a careful mother, before her child goes forth into the damp night air, wraps it in close and warm vestments, so our merciful Redeemer will give us a name of endearment to show us his love before he takes us so near Satan's seat that temptations will come, and sore trials befall. As soon as the figure changes from the incorruptible word of God, that no evil ones may touch successfully, to living human beings who may fall under the wiles of the devil, we see the agencies of wickedness, in plain view, seeking their destruction.

While the good sower sowed good seed, which grew up children of the kingdom, his enemy sowed seed soon after, in the same field, that produced his own likeness, and became children of the devil. The one was wheat; the other tares. The one was nutritious and life-sustaining; the other innutritious and valueless. The one has a market value in all the world; the other is as the chaff driven before the wind. The psalmist compares the righteous to a strong and beautiful tree planted by the rivers of water, while the unrighteous are as the lightest chaff, which the lightest wind of heaven will move from its place. The prodigal son, as a sinner, was fed on the husks of bitter berries left by the swine. In this parable the children of the devil are the fruit of the tares sown at midnight in a spirit of enmity to all goodness—secretly, while all men slept—and the fruit, as might be expected, is evil, and only evil, continually. Tares are a bastard production, resembling corn or wheat, and growing up with them, promising fruit, but never yielding a single grain of value. So the wicked in the Church and in the world are found daily among the children of God, with a seeming prospect and promise of having a religious life; but the Lord knoweth them that are his.

Concerning the sowing of the tares, the Lord said: "An enemy hath done this." The enemy that sowed them was the devil. Let us learn the character of the devil from the word of God.

It is some show of kindness in the friends of the devil to deny his personality. They have not seen him, they say. He is only a principle. Neither have they seen God, nor angel, nor spirit, nor their own soul. Are these only principles, and not individuals? They see the works of the devil every day. No works are more manifest in all the world. They are in us and about us. They are in our neighbors and our children. They are potential and daring. Evidently they are the work of a person, and not a principle. But leaving such idle speculations, as infidelity asserts, we appeal to the word of God as the highest authority known among men.

The Scriptures present the devil before us with many an *alias*. To-day an angel of light; to-morrow an emissary of darkness. Ever changing, he must be named according to his hues. Many of his distinguished followers, who venture upon large crimes, imitate his example, and when detected and indicted for offenses, it is found that in one city they bore one name, in the next which they visited another; and so continuing, they have to be recognized not by their names, which are legion, and have to be stated in the indictment as A B, *alias* C D, *alias* E F, but they are best known by their appearance, speech, address, and the like. The paternity of this trick is in their father, the chief devil. In heaven his name was Lucifer; in hell it is Beelzebub, the prince of the devils. On earth he is called the serpent, the tempter, the devil, Satan, Apollyon, the prince of the power of the air, the wicked one, and by various other names. We do not doubt that Isaiah, in his reference to Lucifer, describes his fall from heaven, as this view is largely supported by many scriptures, which speak of evil spirits in the world acting in opposition to good spirits. So in the beginning we are considering a being who is full of cunning and enmity to our race, who has many to aid and abet him in all wickedness, and who has the knowledge and experience of three worlds—heaven, earth, and hell.

The history of a personal devil is found near the beginning of both Testaments, and soon after man was created, as described in the Old Testament, and soon after Jesus had begun his public ministry, as described in the New. In the first account he is called the serpent; in the second the tempter. He is the same person, but he already appears with an *alias* affixed. He was the first to contemn the government of God. "God," he would say, "is a deceiver, and instead of holding you to an accountability, as he pretends, he knows well enough that as soon as you eat the forbidden fruit your eyes will be opened, and you will be as gods." He preached the first heresy, and he and his followers have never been orthodox to this day. "Ye shall not surely die," was the flat contradiction of the word of the Lord, which had said, "Ye shall surely die." With four thousand years' experience as the tempter, he boldly assailed the Son of God to ruin him. Forty days of preparation by hunger were allowed to the tempter the better to prepare Jesus for a spirit of distrust of God; but this long period of fasting only made him full of grace. In the wilderness, on a pinnacle of the temple, and on an exceedingly high mountain, he plied again and again his hellish darts. In the wilderness he could say: "Adam was alone when he fell; here Jesus is alone, and may fall."

On a pinnacle of the temple he could say: "Adam fell in the holy garden; Jesus may fall in the holy city." And on the mountain he could say: "Adam worshiped me in Eden; Jesus may bend the knee a little in this place, where, in one view, he can see and have offered to him the kingdoms of the world and the glory of them." Adam fell; but, blessed be God, Jesus withstood all the temptations of the tempter. A personal and wicked enemy, named the devil, sowed the tares.

Some suppose that the Book of Job was written first of all the books of the Bible. In the first chapter the devil appears among the sons of God, and in the immediate presence of God. Another *alias* is given to him in the description. With Adam and Eve he was called the serpent, with Christ the tempter, and with Job Satan. He is a personal devil still, seeking to destroy Job. His evil designs may be seen in the dissolute lives of Job's children, and in his utter destruction of them and of all Job's property. The whole mischief produced by Satan in the account is not so unusual in the fact of its occurrence among men as in the fact of its finding a place in the sacred record.

Why is it that such disposition to injure others is found in the devil? We answer, "Like begets its like." The truly good seek to make all others good. The wicked strive to reduce to their own plane of wickedness every particle of virtue and goodness found in any accountable creature. We see bad men daily whose conversation and conduct are constantly tending to destroy every good quality in others, and to make them vile as themselves. It is this evil disposition which makes it so dangerous for our children to associate with bad children. As all begin life with a depraved nature, we find that wickedness strikes into the heart as quickly as a spark ignites powder. It is with great pains that we induce our children to be good from principle, but just a whistle on the street from the vicious takes effect instantly.

A few scriptures will set in strong light the personality and malignity of the devil. We have no account that he ever seeks to change the character or course of the wicked; but it is said with emphasis that if it were possible he would deceive the very elect. Paul calls the devil the god and the prince of this world. He is the ruler of all wickedness. He is "the prince of the power of the air, the spirit that *now* worketh in the children of disobedience." Let any who may flatter themselves that the spirit of the devil does not at the present time effectually influence the spirits of men to wickedness consider the emphasis of the word *now* in this quotation. In one of our Lord's famous conversations with the Jews he presents this subject in all its fearful truth in his answer to them in the following words: "Ye are of your father, the devil, and the lusts of your father ye will do. He was a murderer from the beginning, and abode not in the truth, because there is no truth in him. When he speaketh a lie, he speaketh of his own, for he is a liar, and the father of it." The chief delight of the devil is to disturb the assemblies of the saints. Two hundred years ago De Foe wrote concerning him, in this respect, these lines, which are as true at this day as they were in his time:

> Whenever God erects a house of prayer,
> The devil always builds a chapel there.
> And 't will be found, upon examination,
> The latter has the largest congregation.

The servants are Christ's ministers and others who help to cultivate the field. It was their duty from seed-time to harvest to see that the good seed grew and ripened. After the devil sows tares in a field he pays no further attention to it, knowing that, like all noxious things, they will grow from the force of their own evil nature. But the good seed require a soil carefully prepared, and an assiduous cultivation every day. For some time the wheat and the tares looked precisely alike. So in the Church the real and nominal Christians for a time have equal reputation for piety. But the careful servants of the householder who, like faithful ministers, watched the growth every day, were the first to detect a difference in the plants. Many a religious formalist and hypocrite thinks that his sins rest secretly in his own bosom; but the truth is his minister knows them too well, and aims many a well-directed shot from the pulpit at those very sins. The timely discovery proved the faithfulness of the servants, and at once the householder laid the blame at the right door, and excused them from any censure. While Noah was a preacher of righteousness to the antediluvian world, he was free from guilt, although the imaginations of the thoughts of the hearts of all around him were evil, and only evil, and that continually. While Lot was faithful he was safe, although ten righteous persons could not be found in all Sodom and Gomorrah.

Our Lord teaches us a valuable lesson in the zeal displayed by the servants, which was not according to knowledge. Certainly at that early time in the season they were not good judges of the tares as distinct from the wheat. They had barely made the discovery that all the products did not come from good seed; and yet, with the imperfect knowledge possessed by them, they were anxious to go into the field and commence an indiscriminate destruction, that they might pluck up the tares. So it may be that a hasty exercise of discipline in the Church to suppress supposed or real errors of doctrine or commission of offenses might, in its effects' be more deleterious than to let the good and bad grow together. The person holding the error may be cured by giving him longer time to study the question. The sinning one may have done the act involuntarily, or only occasionally, before it has grown into a habit that will not or cannot be broken. The offender may be so connected with others who are the very salt of the earth that serious disturbances would be created by the ejection. If a careful inspection should enable the tares generally to be rooted up rather than the wheat, still, in some instances, the wheat would suffer. And so, all things considered, it is best that both shall grow together until harvest, and then an exact discrimination will be made between the precious and the vile. The lesson is not against the enforcement of discipline in individual cases where that alone will effect a cure, but it is against a rash and hasty zeal in punishing communities or multitudes of evil persons who associate with the good.

The reapers are the angels who shall be sent forth at the end of the world to gather all the tares into bundles for punishment. Into bundles; how expressive! May it not be that sinners will be collected by classes, that their favorite sins may be seen in all their odiousness? Ten thousand times ten thousand gamblers doomed together and at once, then as many drunkards, then as many liars, then as many scoffers, then as many lovers of pleasure more than lovers of God, and so continuing until all that offend and do iniquity are hurled by the strong angels into the nethermost hell.

No messengers more fit than the angels can be found in the universe to execute justice according to the will of God. Their strength and activity enable them to accomplish the work. Only one of two angels rained fire from heaven upon Sodom and Gomorrah. One angel took Peter from prison, not heeding bars or bolts. The good angels are specially acquainted with the fallen angels, having seen them thrust out of heaven. Jude says: "The angels which kept not their first estate, but left their own habitation, he hath reserved in everlasting chains under darkness unto the judgment of the great day." Very many accounts are found in the Bible of the holy angels being sent on various missions to our world, and there is not an instance of hesitation, delay, or failure on their part in doing the will of God. In the weakest day that Jesus saw on the earth, he declared that he could then pray to his Father, who would send twelve legions of angels to his assistance. By the power of angels he could have swept the earth in an instant of time of all its inhabitants. The angel who rolled away the stone from his tomb could have brought blindness or death upon all Jerusalem.

The chief doctrine taught in this parable is that while men may not judge and destroy one another, yet God watches the good and the bad with an exact providence, referring the deeds of every day to a day of final account.

The Tares.

Not a sparrow falleth on the ground without the notice of God. Even the hairs of our head are all numbered. He never changes any view of right or wrong. His principles of conduct are as immutable as his nature. The end he sees from the beginning. Light and darkness are the same to God. Events are never forgotten or passed by, and in his book of remembrance, which records them all, there is not a single blot or erasure. All things are open and visible to the eyes of Him with whom we have to do. While the enemy that sowed the tares chose the night for its secrecy to sow them, and then went his way imagining that his evil work was unknown, yet the All-seeing Eye observed it, read the sentence of condemnation for the wickedness, saw the evil product growing long before the servants made the discovery, knew that his own seed which he had sown were good, anticipated the righteous anger of the servants before it existed, prepared an answer to their request, and beheld the future harvest—the good saved, the wicked lost.

To the wicked, the doctrine of a special providence that oversees all the affairs of men with reference to a general judgment in the future, when all the thoughts, words, and deeds of the whole life shall be brought into exact and equitable adjudication on their merits, must be a fearful apprehension. In this view it was no poetic indulgence of the apostle when he said, "It is a fearful thing to fall into the hands of the living God." On the other hand, to the righteous there can be no more consoling reflection than the certainty that God sees approvingly every step taken of a faithful life. While he disclaims all merit for every good deed done, and knows that his salvation is of grace, yet his heart rejoices in the knowledge that all his work is for a Master who never fails to reward the deserving. Could we believe and realize constantly that all our actions come before God for inspection and future judgment, how guarded would be our conduct in comparison with our present thoughtlessness. Certainly we show by our frequent forgetfulness of God and our duty that, while we may not directly deny the doctrine here stated, it is practically ignored. No doubt the wicked fondly hug the delusion to their breasts that God is not concerned about the little affairs of their lives; but in this mistake they neither consider the nature of God—from which it is plain that he takes cognizance of all things, and that without reference to great and small as these qualities appear to us—nor do they heed his word, which declares that he searches the thoughts and intents of the heart. On the other hand, a Christian, who should live in close and daily communion with God, studying his nature and his will, should never lose sight of the consolation that his very life is hid with Christ in God.

As a matter of reasoning, one of the strongest persuasions that there will be a future judgment arises from the unsettled state of affairs in this world. Remembering that God discriminates between right and wrong; that his government is over all his creatures; that he completes all that he undertakes; that in this life he has left men free to choose between holiness and sin; that the whole of life is spent frequently by the wicked in successful evasions of the declared will of Heaven, while the righteous as often live and die in poverty and pain, without receiving any known reward for their good conduct—we are not at liberty to believe that this life is the final settlement of human affairs. All nations and peoples, whether civilized or barbarous, intelligent or ignorant, Christian or pagan, have faith in a judgment beyond this life that amounts to a universal persuasion of the fact. But it is only from knowledge obtained through the Scriptures that we learn certainly the accurate observation of God over all human affairs, which he keeps in memory with a view to their final settlement according to the strictest equity, moderated by a Father's love.

The main duty taught in this parable is that we are not to separate from the world, but we are to remain in it according to the will of God, bearing with the froward and the wicked, and seeking to do good to all men.

Our Saviour never shunned a company of bad men. He prayed and wept over Jerusalem when the chief authorities were planning to take his life. He opened the eyes of the blind and unstopped the ears of the deaf without asking whether the persons were saints or sinners. He loved his friends and forgave his enemies. As we are describing one of the imitable perfections of Christ, let us all follow the bright example.

Example is the best teacher. In a certain town an infidel had successfully silenced all opposition to his sinful errors except with one poor shoe-maker. This man had no learning, but he was full of the grace of God. Again and again the wily and learned infidel plied him with sophistries attacking the Christian religion. The constant and only answer of the shoe-maker was, "I know that the love of God is shed abroad in my heart by the Holy Spirit." Watching his daily conduct, the infidel saw that this man governed his life by kindness in his family, industry to support them, charity toward all his neighbors, and every virtue that our holy religion inculcates. After spending several years in fruitless efforts to move the fidelity of the poor man, one day in an experience-meeting at church, to the surprise of all, the infidel arose and said: "I am a convert to Christianity. My change is not caused by any persuasion of truth gathered from the pulpit or from books. I could have lived and died an infidel if it had not been for one man. My neighbor, the shoe-maker, sitting yonder is the man who has rescued me from the bottomless pit. His constant and uniform testimony that the grace of God had saved him, and his daily walk and conversation, which I have observed for years, have forced me to acknowledge that there is a divine reality in his religion. Henceforth his God shall be my God, and his people my people."

All separation from the world with a view to extraordinary purity is sinful, and unauthorized by the word of God, although it may be attended with vows, and ceremonies, and strange vestments, and an order having a holy name. We are to serve every man, woman, and child within our reach, standing ready at all times to help those to whom we do not have daily access as opportunity may give us the privilege; and we are constantly to engage in sending messages of love to the ends of the earth in the name of Jesus. This cannot be done if we inclose ourselves in monastic walls. It cannot be well done if we, in a spirit of bigotry, so love and laud our own Church as to suppose that salvation is found exclusively within its pale. It cannot be well done if we exclude the large liberality of the gospel of Christ by attaching salvation to a mode, or by making a mode the test of Christian communion or Church-fellowship. It cannot be well done under the belief that God has from eternity chosen certain persons to salvation by name and number, irrespective of good works, and by the same decree consigned the rest of mankind by name and number to the pains of eternal death. It cannot be well done by ignoring the work of the Holy Spirit in conviction, regeneration, and sanctification, by supposing that ability and merit are found in our own works to save our souls.

Like our Master, we must live with sinners and labor with sinners. No separation can take place until we reach heaven. The tares and the wheat must grow together, and the final disposal of the two will be made when the angels come and gather the tares in bundles for destruction, transplanting the wheat into the garners of the heavenly world. Duty now and duty discharged with sinners, however painful or prolonged, and however ill received, must be done in this pilgrimage.

The Barren Fig-tree.

"A certain man had a fig-tree planted in his vineyard; and he came and sought fruit thereon, and found none. Then said he unto the dresser of his vineyard, Behold, these three years I come seeking fruit on this fig-tree, and find none: cut it down; why cumbereth it the ground? And he answering said unto him, Lord, let it alone this year also, till I shall dig about it, and dung it; and if it bear fruit, well; and if not, then after that thou shalt cut it down." Luke xiii. 6–9.

PUNISHMENT is not always proof of guilt. Certain Galileans who may have been guilty, or who may have been innocent, under the order of Pilate, had their blood taken from them, which was mingled with the sacrifices. This was done in the temple itself. Possibly the Jews brought the story to Jesus to see what he would say about the Galileans, whom they despised. It was a lamentable tale to be repeated in the ears of those who had many friends in Galilee. The Master received the account and, without denying it, offset it with another story of eighteen persons who lost their lives by the falling of a tower in Siloam. The question raised in both stories was, whether punishment was proof of guilt. The decision of Christ was that suffering may fall upon the guilty or innocent; but in either event those who suffer are not sinners above all others, but that the accusers then before him were sinners, and with an extraordinary emphasis he proclaimed to them, "Except ye repent, ye shall all likewise perish." Repentance lies at the beginning and foundation of all true religion, and is an indispensable prerequisite; and if these religionists standing before him had omitted true repentance, it would avail them nothing to raise questions about Pilate's government, but they would as certainly perish if they lived and died in that state as it was certain that the Galileans had perished under the order of Pilate, or that the eighteen named lost their lives by the falling of the tower in Siloam.

From this interview it was easy and appropriate to introduce before the retailers of news and superficial professors of religion the parable of the barren fig-tree. Whether applied to their nation or themselves, or any formal Church or individual member, a fig-tree, planted, cultivated, full of leaves and limbs and vitality, and yet barren year after year, would be an exact likeness.

As usual we begin with the figures employed.

A certain man—God. Here we have God as Creator and Owner of all things. The history is begun and continued maintaining his rights as absolute and unlimited. He planted a fig-tree, and it became his own. His right was the more undoubted because it was planted in his vineyard. The dresser of the vineyard was his dresser, and he appointed him to cultivate this tree as his own work. The time belonged to him, and he gave abundance of it to allow the fig-tree to grow. The fruit when ripe and gathered would be his own, as he owned all that was necessary in producing the fruit. So God appears here as Creator and absolute Owner.

The rebellion of the heart of man is greater in opposing absolute ownership on the part of God than in any other thing. Many men would be religious if they could have a division of honor and merit between themselves and God in their salvation. If God would furnish all the means and give all the knowledge and power necessary to a religious life—which he does furnish of necessity and grace in every instance—and then reward the poor dependent with pay and praise for every good thing done by him, the heart would at once be flattered by receiving such a religion. But God is a jealous God, and will never divide his honor and glory with another. And far better is it for us that these should be left with our Heavenly Father. A young and inexperienced prodigal may often wish that his estate was in his own hands and out of the control of a careful and prudent guardian; but his own desire granted would soon be his ruin. Our safety is in God. Our rebellion against his absolute ownership in our bodies, property, lives, and eternal interests, if heeded, would soon work our ruin, as we would be wholly incompetent to manage such vast treasures.

On human modes of calculation God has the right to absolute ownership in man and all his possessions. A farmer plows the ground, and he feels that his right to the harvest is increased with the seed sown, the labor bestowed, the care and watchfulness employed, and the grain gathered and placed in the garner. A painter does not set much store to the canvas when it is first prepared for the pencil, but when months and years have passed, and the creations of his genius are seen in every line, and mind and heart have been exerted to their utmost strength, he regards the work as his own and of incalculable value. A young man spends half a decade in learning a profession or a trade, and he justly considers that he is entitled to pay for his skill as well as his labor in all the work of his life. By industry and economy, when two-score years have passed, a man finds himself in possession of an estate sufficient for the support of his family and himself in old age, and he would revolt at the suggestion that his title to it was no better than the title of the man who had never employed one hour in thought or labor for his possessions. And so of all our employments—care and labor give an acknowledged right to our earnings.

In a much larger sense has God been employed in our happiness and welfare, and is therefore the owner of the work of his hands. He is not only Creator, equaling the painter who made the canvas immortal by his genius, but in the most absolute sense he has given us our whole being. Far beyond the claim of the man who tills the ground is the claim of God, as ground, soil, seed, atmosphere, sunshine, rain, and every thing necessary to production, came from his hand.

The kind of nature possessed by every living thing is the provision and gift of God. Here the Lord is without a rival. In ten thousand times ten thousand varieties he has made his creatures to live and be happy. The only disturbance of universal felicity is caused by sin. No greater or more interesting study can be pursued by man than to learn something of the singular nature of beasts, birds, and insects. He will find an immense amount of happiness among them in the midst of the shortest lives and the greatest dangers. He will find in the same species a similarity of nature and disposition in every one so nearly alike as to mark well the species, and at the same time such contrariety when compared with others as at once distinguishes them from all the rest. What amazing wisdom and power of God are necessary to all these results! With what adoring gratitude should we contemplate all his mercies! His title to all things is unlimited and undisputed.

A fig-tree—each individual.

If we can raise the figure in our minds from an unconscious fig-tree to a conscious and intelligent man, and then look first at his surroundings as they are given him of the Lord, and again at his opportunities and capabilities of improvement and doing good, growing out of these surroundings, we shall be able to appreciate the teaching in this part of the parable. Every man has an influence—some limited and some extensive. One can manage only one talent well, while another can use five or ten. But to the extent of the circle of that influence there is a work which each man can do, and no other can do for him. For this work, he is responsible in two worlds—here in the present pilgrimage, there in eternity. He finds many days of his life wherein sickness, youth, and old age leave him unable to work. An absolute uncertainty exists in his own mind as to how many days he may be able to do the will of God. Again, he perceives that no day ever returns with the second offer of time, and that every opportunity to do good is a new one, and not an old one repeated. From these considerations a sensible and sane man will be impressed with the value of the statement, "Now is the accepted time, now is the day of salvation." He will stress *now*.

Personal responsibility will be felt if we will remember that all the figures in the parable relate to the fig-tree—the individual. It was a fig-tree that a certain man planted, caring for it specially. It was a planted fig-tree, with labor and care, and not one growing wild. He planted the fig-tree in his vineyard, and not outside of the inclosure, so that it could have all needed and possible protection. The soil was selected that was adapted to its growth, and well prepared. The planting was done at the right time of the year to produce the best results. The rain, the atmosphere, and the sun all contributed to its welfare. A dresser competent to the work was appointed to attend to it during all the months of the year, who had no other work to do. So in all these particulars do we see that the fig-tree—the individual—is the one cared for above all others, and the one responsible every day. There is no intimation in the Scriptures that our Lord would not have died as freely for one man had he alone descended from Adam, as he has died for the millions of his race. There is no intimation in the Scriptures that each man is less responsible for the conduct of his life because of the vast numbers redeemed and appointed to work in the vineyard, than if only one were called to do the whole work of life.

The leaves in the figure may be considered as part of the fig-tree. They were showy and pretentious, but being without fruit they were valueless. They bedecked and ornamented the fig-tree as if for Sunday attire, but that was all. There was no fruit —not one fig in the midst of ten thousand leaves.

The Master one day came to a fig-tree, and it is said he found nothing thereon but leaves only, and he commanded, "Let no fruit grow on thee henceforward forever." O how many churches do we enter, and how many members do we find who are clothed only with leaves! They are as destitute of inward purity and holiness as were our first parents of all clothing, except fig-leaves—the very figure now under consideration. Look at that pew where father, mother, and children are sitting, clothed in purple and fine linen; but look at the heart, and behold a cage of unclean birds; look at the mind, and each one "leans his idiot back on folly's topmost twig." A great shade is made by this fig-tree, but it only cumbers the ground. A wide range of evil influence is exerted by professors of religion who bear leaves without fruit; but it is a savor of death unto death. "One sinner destroyeth much good."

The vineyard—the Church.

In this place the Church represents the whole body of religious communicants, with its Bible, its ministers, its altars, and its sacraments. It is the Church in its largest sense. Every small congregation, where only two or three are gathered together and where worship is conducted, is part of the universal Church, and each member stands personally identified with all. Citizenship in the Church is much larger than citizenship in the State.

In the Church, there is neither Jew nor Greek; in the State, the lines are fixed and the jurisdiction limited. We are born into the State without choice or privilege; we choose the Church, and are born into God of our own free will and desire. Where the Spirit of the Lord is, there is liberty.

A decisive proof that the Church is the peculiar organization of God in this world is found in the fact that, while it lives on the voluntary principle, it survives all opposition in all the centuries. The motto of holiness, inscribed as the chief motto on the banners of the Church, has at all times provoked the deadly hostility of an unregenerate world. Never have such efforts been made to destroy any cause as have been made to destroy the Church of God. Unless it had been from heaven, its destruction had been secured long ago. No human institution attempts to stand against formidable opposition without calling in help from others and securing strength by alliances. But the Church moves forward proclaiming "peace on earth, good-will toward men," trusting solely in the protection of Heaven, and to-day it is stronger than ever before. The Arm Unseen that moves the world must be its support.

Of all organizations known to our race the Church is the oldest. It is certain that profane history does not pretend to name the beginning of the Church. If it could do so, this would be an unanswerable argument to prove that the Church is of man and not of God. Its origin is before the beginning of reliable human records, and the Bible is the only book that contains its history. In the family of Adam an altar for worship was erected. Noah was a preacher of righteousness, and built an altar to God. Abraham, Isaac, and Jacob had their altars to God for themselves, their families, and their dependents. Moses officiated in the Church in the wilderness. David praised God in the sanctuary with heart and lips and instruments. In New Testament times the Church was in the wilderness and in the city, in the home and in the synagogue. The last book of the Bible contains separate addresses to the seven churches of Asia. The Church has an ancient, a modern, a warlike, and a peaceful history; but appearing in all the centuries as the child of God.

We profess a tender affection for all the branches of the Church of Christ. While some doctrines are unscriptural, and some practices unreasonable, and many members bring a reproach on the holy cause, and preachers can be found who serve for the loaves and fishes, yet in them all there are godly men and women, and in each division more than seven thousand who have not bowed the knee to Baal. With most devout and unselfish feelings do we love to contemplate this "army of the living God," thinking of each division as it fights the good fight of faith," and of each one triumphant in the "swellings of Jordan," and meeting and greeting the redeemed of the Lord on the other side, where there is no occasion to sing:

> Let party names no more
> The Christian world o'erspread;
> Gentile and Jew, and bond and free,
> Are one in Christ their head.

The dresser—the minister and pastor of the Church.

"Then said he unto the dresser of his vineyard"—showing that the dresser was called and appointed to the work, that by study and experience he was qualified for it, and that his relation to the owner of the vineyard was most intimate and mutually confiding. At once we see the character of the ministers of Christ. Like other soldiers, they do not go on a warfare at their own charges. God appoints and sends, and the Church receives and supports. How can they preach except they be sent? Are they not embassadors of Christ? Even in human governments citizenship makes no one an embassador, but an appointment by the chief executive and the great seal of the State are necessary. The Christian minister does not parade his parchments on every street as the proof of his call, but he points rather to the slain of the Lord under his ministry and to those made every whit whole. He proclaims life to all men and in all places. He alone of all men carries an open mission of love to every son and daughter of Adam.

There is not a period recorded in the Scriptures in which God did not have holy men in charge of his Church. These men have truly been the light of the world. To cry aloud and spare not, denouncing sin and commanding holiness, has been their employment. Next to the family relation, theirs is the most delicate and responsible known among the families of men. Instructing the young, comforting the sick, baptizing and giving the holy communion to all, and preaching the unsearchable riches of Christ, are such duties as lead the minister to the inner door of the hearts of men. How loving, how wise, how prudent should he be! It was amazing love, when God said, "Cut it down," that the dresser dared to intercede, and by importunate prayer had the life of the fig-tree prolonged one entire year. Let us ask and esteem the prayers of our ministers. The effectual, fervent prayer of a righteous man availeth much.

It is no wonder that the men of the world regard the ministry as a very ineffectual agency to bring the nations to know Christ. None of God's ways have ever accorded with their imaginary wisdom. They are very sure that a better Bible could be prepared if the Lord were its author; and yet none of their books, in any one leading feature, can bear a comparison. They feel certain that if God had intended them as free moral agents, and liable to future punishment for disobedience in this life, he would have made their duty and their immortality and a place called hell plainer than they are; but when they try to make a substitute, leaving this pilgrimage one of faith and trial, they cannot compete with the certainty which the Lord has furnished. They show their own party by the *best* men in it; they judge the Church by its *worst* men. And so they regard the ministry as a feeble organization and altogether of the world. But when they look at the results of preaching the gospel, without civil or military power to support it, and in the face of the natural disinclination of men to receive it, they will search in vain for some human work that has accomplished as much under like circumstances. But by the foolishness of preaching, as men esteem it, God has chosen to convert the world. Let no one mistake this for foolish preaching, but let all ministers be wise as serpents and harmless as doves.

The doctrine of the parable is the long forbearance of God connected with the constant demands of justice. The forbearance of God makes many say, Where is the promise of his coming? Do not all things remain as they were from the foundation of the world? The fig-tree was capable of bearing fruit when it was first planted, and it was for this object alone that it was planted. What a vast mercy to prolong its days three years, when nothing but leaves were found in any year! The inference was easily drawn that such forbearance was proof of continued forbearance; and in this expectation of indulgence fig-tree and dresser were only awakened by the startling demand of justice that never slumbers nor sleeps, "Cut it down."

Men are very inconsistent when they demand instant punishment for sins committed against themselves, and then complain of God for any delay in punishment, and more for any punishment after a period of delay, and still more for providing a way of pardon for the guilty so as to escape punishment. With men it is first a declaration of war, and then instantly following the boom of the cannon and the certainty of death. But God is long-suffering and full of compassion, and from this men infer that justice will sleep forever. In their own government justice must stand with drawn sword to protect the good and punish the wicked. But the pleasing and illusory thought is indulged that in the government of God sin is as safe as holiness, and that all will receive the same destiny in eternity. O infamous cheat of the devil when he said, in his first approach to our Federal Head, "Ye shall not surely die!" The flattering belief that death is always distant, and eternal death only a fiction, leads many a soul to hell. The utmost that justice would allow was that after the trial of one year if no fruit appeared the whole tree should be cut down. And to the impenitent reader of these lines we say there is an uncertain last year of merciful visitation and waiting in his life to bear fruit, after which there will be found no place for repentance, although he seek it with tears.

The forbearance of God is long continued when we consider in how short a time his will can be done as to the main duty of life. The main duty of life is found in obedience to this command, "Seek ye first the kingdom of God." Be truly religious before you eat or sleep. If your father be dead, do not wait to bury him before you give your heart to Christ; but let the dead bury their dead. Now, this initial act of religion can be accomplished in an hour; and for that hour God often waits threescore years. Is not this truly long-suffering on the part of God? What grievous sins the eyes of our Heavenly Father must have beheld in all the years of a long pilgrimage, each one pointing to punishment and death! And yet with true paternal solicitude God waited another and another year to see if any fruit would be borne in that wasted life.

Work to produce fruit is the duty taught in the parable.

Consider the immense evil done by a fig-tree cultivated three years without fruit. The dresser has expended three years of labor on it without profit, when he might have been employed in a vineyard where each tree would bring forth fruit thirty, sixty, or a hundred fold. The rain, the sunshine, and the atmosphere have been employed in abundance for the good of this tree without any returns. The large and attractive leaves of the tree have only furnished a shade to retard the growth of other vegetation. The roots of the tree have penetrated the earth and absorbed the soil quite a distance, injuring every thing that grows in its neighborhood. Labor and time and money and place are all lost on the unsuccessful attempt to produce only one fig on a tree capable of bearing for three years. All this train of thought applies with force to the ungodly. By word and by example they have done evil, and that continually. Hundreds of sermons have been preached at their hearts, all missing their aim. Living forty-nine years, the sinner has had seven years of Sabbaths—a period of time sufficiently long to learn any trade or profession. In good influences he has not produced one fig. Often has the stern voice of justice cried, "Cut him down!" but the tender and pleading voice of mercy prevailed, and he was spared another year.

"Son, go work to-day in my vineyard." The words are kind and authoritative. To-day can never mean to-morrow. Care and work enough will to-morrow have when it comes; and sufficient unto the day is the evil thereof. No one can ever recover the loss who has lost a day. It is an unjust imposition on the future to expect it to carry the load of the past.

Any work is easier done at the time when it should be performed than at any after time. One of the most unfortunate habits of life into which many people fall is the habit of delay in beginning at once to do the work of the day. The thoughts concerning it, and the apprehension of labor and fatigue, at least equal the trouble of the performance with one who begins in earnest and continues until the work is done. We strongly advise all young people to form the habit in early life of entering upon every duty without a moment's hesitation, whether it be temporal or spiritual work; and in securing the certain salvation of the soul, let no hinderance prevent a full and immediate acceptance of Christ.

In human affairs, all compensation is determined by the amount and quality of labor done. Why should this principle be regarded as strange in the government of God? If a man shall say he has faith when he is destitute of works, his avowal is disproved by his life. A good tree will bring forth good fruit. One who has tasted that the Lord is good will desire that others should be partakers of the same blessing. The merit of works and works as a test of faithfulness are very different things. All merit is in Christ; all loyalty is shown in doing his will. We should even strive to do his will on earth as it is done in heaven, with like love and constancy.

> My drowsy powers, why sleep ye so?
> Awake, my sluggish soul!
> Nothing has half thy work to do,
> Yet nothing's half so dull.

THE DISCOVERIES OF SIN.

"Be sure your sin will find you out." Num. xxxii. 23.

NO greater difficulty is found in the pulpit than to make the hearers feel that they are the guilty ones alluded to in the sermon. No little stratagem is necessary to make David feel, even under Nathan, "Thou art the man." A *direct* approach is often a failure because it is resisted; an *indirect* because it is misapplied. We are apt to believe that we know our *neighbor's sins* better than our own.

The text is *personal,* and the sermon must be likewise. If any one transfers it to his neighbor, the influence is lost. A man said to us once: "I liked your sermon to-day; it was so *general.*" We intended it for him, and we felt ashamed of the result. Preaching at Rockcastle Springs a very practical sermon, several hearers approached us after service and asked if we meant *a certain man,* a stranger, whom we barely knew. We really meant *the inquirers.*

We are all enough alike in our native depravity and sinful acts to be portrayed in this faithful text.

As in water face answereth to face, so the heart of man to man. Sin never changes. It begins in guilt, and ends in death. The word of God is a bright and truthful mirror for beholding ourselves, and all its virtues will be lost if we keep turning it on others so as to behold only them. Let us not hesitate to-day to look at the picture as being like ourselves, and then when we leave this house let us not straightway forget what manner of men we are. Be certain that your sin will find you out if it continues, and that your own forgetfulness or transfer will not conceal your guilt or lessen the danger.

1. It is *your* sin.

Every one loves *his own wrong-doing*, and can see but little harm in it. His own evil ways soon become his easily besetting sin. His love for his own evil course is shown in the great number of times that he repeats the same things. The old sinner's eye brightens as he looks back on the sinful days of early life, and he wishes he were young again that he might renew its pleasures. It was a long course of voluntary sin before the prodigal could be brought to say, "I have sinned against heaven, and in thy sight." And so of David, when he was at last compelled to say, "Against thee, thee only, have I sinned."

Each sin is *popular*, and has a large following. There are abundance of tastes for every sin. Nothing is learned so rapidly as to sin, and nothing is seized upon with such avidity. A whistle brings the sinners together on the street—no argument or persuasion necessary. Satan has neither a Bible for instruction, a house for worship, sermons for conviction, hymns for praise, nor prayers for help. His cause is readily espoused without such aids.

The guilt of sin is found in its *voluntary* character. No decree or necessity of nature compels a man to sin. We are not to lay our sins either upon Adam or our neighbor, as they are our own. Adam blamed the woman, and the woman the serpent, and the serpent would have sought to transfer the guilt if he could have found another, so prone are we to deny our guilt and to blame others. We sin only as far as we choose to sin. We desist as soon as we are willing to desist. Even Satan cannot drive us beyond our choice. It is all a mistake that sinful habits are so confirmed that they cannot be broken. The inebriate who ceases to drink for a week or a month gives plain proof that he could desist longer if he would. It is our own sin that we roll under our tongue as a sweet morsel. If it were another's, we would not love it so well. It is so eminently our own sin that God holds us responsible for all the deeds done in the body, as if we alone had received the benefits of Christ's death. No thought more affecting than this: Christ would have died for *me* alone. Then for *my sin* committed against such a Saviour I am properly punished.

What a picture of a misspent life to think that a man has lived all his days in willing sins of his own in violation of the laws of God and man, risking eternal punishment contrary to the teachings of his own conscience and judgment, liable to lose heaven, without any hope of reward, to the injury of all his powers, and when virtue, religion, peace, reward, joy, and eternal life were offered to him on the easy condition that he would depart from iniquity, cease to do evil, and learn to do well!

2. *Your sin* will *find you out.*

Our secret sins—and how much more our public sins!—are in the light of God's countenance, and he cannot look upon sin with allowance or approbation; hence, seen by him they will be known. He records them, and his book never changes. But they are soon brought to the light where others see them. Adam and Cain were the first sinners, and their deeds were not hidden for a day. So of David before Nathan, of Ananias and Sapphira, of Simon the sorcerer, and of Judas Iscariot. Often they are known before we are aware of the detection. Many a man walks the streets supposing that his true character of guilt is unknown to the town, and at the same time even the children know his evil manner of life.

All men are willing that the sins of others should be known, and they help to discover them. Indeed, the whole world is full of sin-discoverers.

The subject is in the conversation of every day; it fills a large space in every newspaper, it is heard in every pulpit, and every court-house and jail points out the detected victims. Those who break the laws of the land are surprised every day at their sudden and unexpected arrest. The testimony on the trial of an offender is often as thrilling as a romance in its incidents of search and discovery. The police, enemies, accomplices, confessions, change of circumstances, and even small hints, lead to the detection. One day Mr. Webster remarked in a famous prosecution, "A thousand eyes are turned every way to discover the crime, and the secret is nowhere safe." Six years' experience as commonwealth's attorney convinced us that no crime was ever planned and executed well in all its parts. It is certain that your sins will find you out, from the fact that no confidence and but little sympathy exists between sinners. They not only betray but they fleece each other all the time. The greater part of the gains of sinners—such as gamblers, whisky-venders, and others—are made out of other sinners. All classes of sinners are unreliable. If a spark of better nature exists, it informs on the worse nature, and strives to rise above a state of guilt.

A sinner's appearance tells the tale. That young man's blood-shot eyes, red nose, thick tongue, and trembling hand show that he has been a frequent visitor to the bottle. What a life of misery is before her if some nice young lady should become his wife! The appearance of a theater-going and dancing woman shows that she is enervated and unfit for domestic life. A sinner's words, as they pass from his mouth, show that he is a sinner. There is something in the face of an extortioner or a miser that shows his wickedness. On the other hand, virtue shines out in the face of the good. A halo of glory is around his charities. True religion seeks no hiding-place for its deeds, nor yet the uppermost seat at feasts to attract attention; its deeds are its praises; it goes about doing good, and its reward is on high. But vice seeks concealment, tries to cover its shame, and denies its guilt.

3. The consequences of *your sin*.

All sinners prefer darkness to light for their deeds, because they are evil. The fact that secrecy is sought for sins and the hiding and denial of them prove the universal conviction that they are wrong. No one advocates sin as a thing *per se* right as he understands sin. Not a book written, not a theory started in its favor; and yet the world is full of it. The cause, the heart *deceitful* above all things. So deceitful is it that the result is seen in the fact that the devil is the only one in the universe who gets a large and willing following without pay or promises. A day's work for bread cannot be done without pay, but a month's debauch is no uncommon thing without fee or reward if Satan wills it.

Sin is an unmixed evil. It never begins, continues, or ends in good. As soon as two sins are added together, they commence seeking a third, and begin their work of injury. Things opposite agree to carry out sin. One had bought a piece of ground, another five yoke of oxen, and a third had married a wife, but each agrees that the other's excuse is valid. But the evil consequences soon appear. It may be the smallest touch on the body, but the evil is perceptible. As there is never any advantage from sin in this life, we must conclude there is none beyond. The same God will regard holiness and sin in eternity as he regards them in time. Sins of the body result in diseases of the body, sins of the mind in mental disturbances of various kinds, and sins of the soul in a decided increase of depravity. The wages of sin is death. God pays men for sinning in this life only in dying, and we may be certain that there will be no other pay in the next world.

The main expense of all the governments of the world is caused by sin. Wars, murders, arson, thefts, and all crimes, are instigated by the devil and charged to the tax-payers. The addition of taxes to support sin would Christianize the world. If it were not for sin, it is probable that the body would become healthy, and that the large majority of people would die of old age; but now the consequences of sin are such that every cemetery marks the uncertainty of death, from the youngest infant to the oldest man. If it were not for sin, every mind would see and know the truth, and every soul would love and worship God.

Each act of sin lasts forever. It can never be blotted out, and its evil effects remain. All sin is committed in opposition to the love, mercy, and goodness of God, and it strikes at every interest of society. We arraign sin, and place it on trial to-day. It is wrong in theory, in example, in practice, in thought, and in word. The injury to body, mind, and soul begins with the first act of sinning, and increases in time and in eternity, unless the cause is taken away and the disease removed. A life of sin is without present or future advantage either in prospect, promise, or reality. A time approaches when there will be no place for repentance.

4. The *cure* for *your sin*.

Nature, physical and moral, cannot cure sin. All physical remedies are intended only for the body. All moral remedies of men fail to reach the soul. No one goes to an earthly physician for medicine to cure sin. Even fame, wealth, and pleasure, so much coveted by men, are not intended for this purpose, and really have a tendency to increase and aggravate the disease. It would be strange if a cure of any complaint should be found where no cure was expected, and where the remedy was evidently ineffectual. The cure for sin lies in the *grace of God*. The grace of God that bringeth salvation hath appeared unto all men. One effectual cure tendered by one Physician is offered in good faith to the whole world. This Physician, Jesus Christ, tasted death for every man, and his blood received in faith is the cure for sin-sick souls.

This remedy is offered to-day. Like any remedy for the body or mind of man, this may be refused and rejected. The penalty for final rejection is the death that never dies. The most horrible conception of the human mind is that of a man who lives here a long life in the guilt and danger of sin, and who dies rejecting the cure, and in hell lifts up his eyes in undying torment. In our Master's name, we beseech you harden not your hearts. Many have been cured—indeed, all who have properly applied; and this should encourage and embolden all to apply to the great Physician. Now is the accepted time.

OUR LORD'S PARABLES.

The Prodigal and the Self-righteous Son.

"A certain man had two sons; and the younger of them said to his father, Father, give me the portion of goods that falleth to me. And he divided unto them his living. And not many days after the younger son gathered all together, and took his journey into a far country, and there wasted his substance with riotous living. And when he had spent all, there arose a mighty famine in that land; and he began to be in want. And he went and joined himself to a citizen of that country; and he sent him into his fields to feed swine. And he would fain have filled his belly with the husks that the swine did eat; and no man gave unto him. And when he came to himself, he said, How many hired servants of my father's have bread enough and to spare, and I perish with hunger! I will arise and go to my father, and will say unto him, Father, I have sinned against heaven, and before thee, and am no more worthy to be called thy son; make me as one of thy hired servants. And he arose, and came to his father. But when he was yet a great way off, his father saw him, and had compassion, and ran, and fell on his neck, and kissed him. And the son said unto him, Father, I have sinned against heaven, and in thy sight, and am no more worthy to be called thy son. But the father said to his servants, Bring forth the best robe, and put it on him; and put a ring on his hand,

and shoes on his feet; and bring hither the fatted calf, and kill it; and let us eat, and be merry; for this my son was dead, and is alive again; he was lost, and is found. And they began to be merry. Now his elder son was in the field; and as he came and drew nigh to the house, he heard music and dancing. And he called one of the servants, and asked what these things meant. And he said unto him, Thy brother is come; and thy father hath killed the fatted calf, because he hath received him safe and sound. And he was angry, and would not go in; therefore came his father out, and entreated him. And he answering said to his father, Lo, these many years do I serve thee, neither transgressed I at any time thy commandment; and yet thou never gavest me a kid, that I might make merry with my friends; but as soon as this thy son was come, which hath devoured thy living with harlots, thou hast killed for him the fatted calf. And he said unto him, Son, thou art ever with me, and all that I have is thine. It was meet that we should make merry, and be glad; for this thy brother was dead, and is alive again; and was lost, and is found." Luke xv. 11–32.

IN this parable we have four characters to consider: (1) God in his kindness and forbearance to the vilest of men, as seen in the man who had two sons; (2) the sinner departing from God, as seen in the first part of the history of the prodigal; (3) the sinner repenting of his sins and finding mercy with God, as seen in the last part of the prodigal's history; (4) the worldly-minded and self-righteous, as seen in the history of the elder son.

1. A certain man—God.

He had two sons, the elder and the younger.

Here we have a clew to the entire subject before us. This man had an ample estate, but he had no larger family than he could support. If his circumstances had been limited and straitened, some pretext for wandering on the part of the prodigal might have been found in the fear that would naturally arise that want might overtake him. How infinite the resources of God! When we consider his wealth in the whole universe, we are left without doubt that he can furnish a heaven for each saint. "In my Father's house are many mansions; were it not so I would have told you. I go to prepare a place for you."

As there were two sons in this family, so God often shows us his goodness under two things represented. In the beginning of the world our Heavenly Father commenced our race with two persons —Adam and Eve. The first religious altar had two brothers—Cain and Abel. Abraham and Lot were two representatives in their day. The Bible has two parts—the Old and New Testament. The Church has two periods—the Jewish and the Christian. It has two sacraments—baptism and the Lord's Supper. Two Sabbaths have been furnished —the last day of the week under the old economy, and the first under the new. Two classes of men are in the world—sinners and saints. Two characters dwell apart from each other in eternity—the lost and the saved.

The Prodigal Son. 105

Our Heavenly Father, under the figure of an earthly father, here shows us his goodness in three ways—in dividing the estate with the sons equally and without a day of delay, in letting the younger have all and depart without one questioning word as to his wisdom in going and using it well, and in following him with his love in all his wanderings.

The personalty of the father was divided equally between the sons without any delay. And is not this like the dealings of God with all his children? He sends the rain on the just and the unjust. He opens his hand and satisfies the desire of every living creature. There is never the delay of an hour after the want exists. We breathe as soon as we are born, for breathing is essential to continued life. The sun shines upon vegetation the first day that it springs out of the earth. The swallow finds its home and its supply of food at the same time. There was no inquiry as to the difference in character of the two brothers. Subsequent developments showed decided differences between the two, but the supply to each was the same. God makes a general provision for all according to their nature—not only to all men, but to all creatures, and that too without reference to good or bad qualities. This universal supply is not any more the result of his unlimited resources than of his infinite goodness. Giving does not impoverish God, neither does withholding enrich him; but he delights in giving, and furnishes to each person on each day enough of good things that he could not otherwise obtain to fill his whole life with obligation. Four times in one Psalm is the language found: "O that men would praise the Lord for his goodness, and for his wonderful works to the children of men!"

It was more remarkable in the father than the gift itself to give his prodigal son one-half of his living without a questioning word or a single doubt as to the judicious use he would make of it. No doubt he had seen painful forebodings of extravagance and waste in this son when he should have the means to gratify their indulgence. If he had not seen these symptoms in the young man, the very manner of his address to his father might well enough excite his apprehensions. The amount given had probably cost the father years of labor and prudent economy to own so much; yet with all these considerations before him, he did not utter a word of inquiry or suspicion. He might have reminded him of his comfortable and life-long home, of the uncertain friendship and fidelity of strangers, and of the danger of wild and evil associates; and he might prudently have asked him where he was going, what calling he would follow, and what were his plans; but, like a trusting father, he did none of these things. How like our Heavenly Father!

All the gifts of God are made on the supposition that we will use them well. In the lap of one man the Lord pours wealth in the most lavish manner. He takes it for granted that this man will take care of the poor around him, and will send the gospel far and near; and does not for a moment think that he will lay up for himself all his wealth as treasures upon earth. To another man is given large knowledge and varied opportunities for its increase; and in no stinted measure is he known to be a man of vast information, while around him are the conditions for exerting an influence possibly world-wide, and all without the least suspicion that they will be abused. The eye that sees, the ear that hears, the tongue that speaks, and the feet that walk are given to men in perfection without any questioning that they will be used well. The child at its mother's knee in prayer is expected by the Lord to be his follower in the morning of life, and he has made no other plan for its conduct in the future. Every person and every creature is given its own nature in perfection without a doubt expressed or implied that its sphere will be well filled.

The sequel shows plainly that the love of the father had followed the son while at home, on leaving home, in every haunt of sin, and in returning to the place where his duty and happiness were to be found. Months and years while the prodigal was gone this love might have remained in his own breast without one expressive word, but as soon as the son was in sight neither his guilt, nor his poverty, nor his rags, nor his bare feet, kept the overwhelming love of the father from manifesting itself. No amount of anger or opposition on the part of the elder son could stop the expression of joy which the father felt for a single hour. He only remembered "my son was dead, and is alive; he was lost, and is found."

It was only a murmur that was the immediate occasion of this parable. In a sly and insinuating manner the scribes and Pharisees attempted to lessen the influence of our Saviour when they had searched in vain for any act of his life or word of his lips that was wrong, by whispering to his prejudice as they were making a show of their piety, "This man receiveth sinners and eateth with them," which was to his praise and not to his dispraise. Then followed the parable of the lost sheep, the lost piece of silver, and the prodigal son, and as underlying them all the heaven-born utterance, "There is joy in heaven in the presence of the angels of God over one sinner that repenteth." The first hour in the life of any man when joy in heaven is recorded in his favor is the hour of his repentance. Only one repenting sinner will produce this joy. So it is not surprising that one returning and repenting prodigal should reänimate the heart of his father with all his former love and solicitude. God desires to hasten the restoration of every sinful soul who seeks his face, by taking him at once into his Church, giving back his home and his possessions, clothing him with the righteousness of faith in Christ, and giving him to eat of that bread of which if a man eat he shall never hunger.

Notice one fact carefully. The prodigal was born a son, and not a stranger or alien. While he inherited his father's physical and moral nature, which embraced, as the sequel showed, the power to sin, yet he was born at home, a son entitled to an estate, protected and beloved. The redemption in Christ Jesus removes the natural forfeiture under Adam. Children dying before overt acts of sin are all saved through Christ, and although depravity attaches to their nature, they are as well prepared for heaven as an adult after regeneration. The highest state of Christian perfection is not a state of grace beyond the condition of an infant by virtue of the atonement of Christ. And if thirty-three years be the average of human life, we may rejoice that probably one-fourth of that period is protected by the blood of Jesus; so that living or dying, the young are saved during these years.

In the order prescribed we notice the prodigal's departure from his father, and the sinner's departure from God.

The proposed separation came from the prodigal. He desired to leave home, no doubt being tired of all advice, restraint, and law. The sinner desires to escape from the eye and justice of God, and to be free without dictation. The father did not propose a separation for any cause. He might have said: "My son, you are of age and free; go, and make your fortune." Or: "You are indolent and indifferent to my interest and your duties; go, and provide for yourself." Every separation of the sinner from the Lord is proposed by the sinner, and every step that widens the separation is made by him. "God willeth not the death of the sinner, but rather that he would turn and live." Whatever evil consequences result from the separation will lie at the door of the sinner, and will be properly chargeable to his account. "Turn ye, turn ye; why will ye die?"

How long time the prodigal had meditated the step he was taking we cannot tell. We only know that he did not counsel with father, brother, or servants. The pleasurable emotions of expected liberty and happiness all glowed within his own heart. He was living in castles in the air never to be occupied. To-morrow and happiness he considered inseparable. Freedom and bliss were with him synonymous terms. But in due time these secret meditations found utterance in the presence of a confiding and loving father.

See how abruptly he approached his father with the subject of his desires: "Father, give me the portion of goods that falleth to me." He does not assign any reason for the formal and forward demand, nor does he ask any advice. He wanted the goods to gratify his pleasures and his lusts. How like every sinner is this example! The prayer of the prodigal is the prayer of the sinner: "Father, give me rain in season, an abundant harvest, a good market, health in my family, strength and reason and long life." And if any of these are withheld for a week or a month, the sinner begins to complain of God. He treats all good as his right, and the visitation of all evil as an unjust punishment. When his desires are gratified, prosperity only hardens his heart, and adversity is sent as the last hope of imparting wisdom. The prodigal asked neither for his brother nor the servants any gift, but desired all for himself. His selfishness was absolute and complete. To tear down old barns and build new ones for himself, that he may have room to bestow his goods, is the aim and delight of every sinner. He cannot brook any delay. He must receive his part at once. His whole life is passed in the anxious inquiry: "What shall I eat, and what shall I drink, and wherewithal shall I be clothed?"

"Not many days after the prodigal gathered all together, and took his journey into a far country." Procrastination appears only in deciding to obey God. To depart from God is simultaneous with the first desire to sin. The prodigal was ready to go the very hour he made the demand, if he had sold all his goods and converted them into money.

But this was a work which required a few days, and they were days of eager desire to leave home for freedom. He only made preparation to leave, and did not seek any advice or ask any parental blessing. He did not inquire whether it was best to travel east, west, north, or south; but to get away was his aim, knowing that every step carried him farther from home and restraint and law. How like the sinner! Freedom and licentiousness are considered synonymous terms, and liberty without law is the only kind desired. Many persons suppose they escape all responsibility to God and his Church by remaining in the world and refusing to assume Church vows and obligations. This is a common and grave mistake. Every man is justly responsible for all the good he could accomplish in the Church, and for all the duties incumbent on him as laid down in the Scriptures; and a voluntary refusal to unite with the Church only increases his guilt. No man can escape the responsibility of citizenship to his country by failing or refusing to vote or to exercise any of the privileges of a citizen.

The natural result to the prodigal was that his journey into a far country ended in wasting his substance in riotous living. He had his desire, but the result in every way was contrary to his expectations. The distance from pleasure to pain on the road of sin is a very short one, and the latter is as certain as the former. The only happy time of the prodigal was in the conception and commencement of his schemes. As certainly as thorns are concealed beneath the brightest roses, sin is followed by punishment in a short time. He made the common mistake that a full purse was inexhaustible. So the sinner thinks that his wealth and his pleasures owned to-day will never fail. Every dollar spent in riotous living lessened his treasures and increased his evil habits. The course of his life was effecting his ruin in two ways at once—lessening his power to provide for himself and increasing his appetite for carnal delights. Many a debauchee realizes the keenness of desire for his favorite pleasure as he expends his last farthing in its gratification more than when he began the indulgence with many thousands unused. The prodigal wasted his very substance in riotous living, and not his small change that he could well spare. He gave up all his possessions, and with them the opportunity and capacity to acquire more. He was too far away from home to ask his father for relief, and his body and mind were too enervated to work for more than a bare subsistence. Many sinners find themselves a wreck in body, mind, and soul by the time they waste their first fresh powers of capacity to work.

How different are sinful companions toward one who is full and the same person when empty! While the prodigal had a full purse and was liberal in its extravagance, flatterers and admirers were around him every day; but when his substance was wasted, he had to seek employment for himself. Possibly the one who gave him the first dram would be the first to forsake him in an hour of inebriety, saying, as he turned away: "Poor fellow! what a pity that he was not more of a man!" As between sinners there is no assurance of continued friendship, but when disastrous changes take place separation is inevitable. The friendship of sinners toward each other is of the most uncertain duration, being liable to be disturbed by the smallest things, and is only secure for an hour when the skies are clear and every earthly event propitious. From worldly friendship to worldly enmity there is only a step, and that taken bitter rancor and hate fill the soul.

Here we are inclined to pause and review the journey of the prodigal, while we inquire at each step, "Why did he wander from home?" When he found his confiding father without one questioning word willing to divide the estate and give him his portion, it seems strange that he did not hesitate to take it, and at once resolve to remain. When he saw the property disturbed and scattered, and the home thrown into confusion by his demand, we would have expected that he would relent. The anxiety and concern on the faces of the household should have softened his heart. When he turned for a moment, if he did turn, to look for the last time on the dear old homestead, where he was born and reared, and where he had never known a day of want, it is wonderful that he could travel any farther toward strangers. When he passed the boundary line of his father's lands, or when he saw the last face that he knew, or when he heard the last sound of his native tongue, and began to hear a strange dialect that he understood not, why did he not on some of these occasions have a better mind and come to himself in time? But no; none of these things moved him for an hour. And how many occurrences in the sinner's pathway of life are found strangely insufficient to turn his heart to God! He hears unmoved appeals from the word of God and from the pulpit to save his soul while he may, but he lives on in sin. He buries father, mother, wife, or child, and thinks for a moment that he will repent; but on the morrow he drinks down iniquity as the thirsty ox drinketh water. He tries the sinful pleasures of the world until body and mind are reduced to the very dregs of capacity, and he proposes feebly a reformation; but evil habits hold him by a strong and unyielding chain. The motives and the opportunities for repentance are scattered along the pathway of the sinner's life, but he may neglect them all, and die unpardoned and without hope.

In every step sin led the prodigal from bad to worse. No improvement is ever made in any step taken in sin. Leaving home the prodigal was found among strangers. From a full purse he soon has an empty one; from congenial companions he passed to miserable solitude; from an easy life to a degrading employment; from plenty to hunger; from the protection and advice of his father at home to the companionship of swine. "The wages of sin is death." "Escape for thy life." "Tarry not in all the plain."

The repenting sinner is next seen in the history.

We now approach a scene of amazing mercy and unexpected change. It is wonderful that one as low as the prodigal could escape from ruin. Many years ago a promising young lawyer in a state of semi-inebriation said to us: "I am going voluntarily down the declivity of respectability and usefulness, and when I reach the foot I will show you how a man can rise in his own strength." We replied: "You will never rise in your own strength if you go farther." He proceeded, and fell forever. His trust was not in God. His own strength was very weakness. The first thoughts of the prodigal were connected with home and his father. At once he looked away from himself.

The first words spoken concerning the prodigal when the first good thoughts entered his heart are worthy of notice. He came to himself. He saw men as trees walking; but it was a great improvement on blindness to see even those. O what memories crowded upon the poor prodigal in a moment!

Innocence, home, favors, association, advice, prayers, wandering, strangers, plenty, want, riotous living, all, all in the first view of the past. Memory was faithful, but it was laden with anguish. To himself he was a wonder and a great grief of mind. One mystery was that he could have fallen so low without being aware that he was falling. How strong must have been the influence of his lusts and the temptations of the devil combined. In all that he had ever done himself there was not one pleasant thought. He was clothed in tattered garments, and his own righteousness appeared as filthy rags. He could say, "I the chief of sinners am." While all the past stood in a stupefied daze to his apprehension, yet he was at the point where "there is joy in heaven in the presence of the angels of God over one sinner that repenteth."

Repentance and prayer were in his first thoughts.

The example here set before the sinner, of acknowledgment of sin and repentance, is worthy of imitation, and is more complete than we generally see. He does not excuse himself or make any statement in his own favor. He looks at his guilt in a double view; he had sinned against heaven, and he had sinned in the sight of his father. The law and government of heaven he had opposed, in every step of his journey and his course, until his sins culminated in guilt in his father's sight. He acknowledged that he had not only forfeited the right to be the son of his father, but he did not expect to be called his son. He sought the place of a servant—even a hired servant who worked a day at a time and left when the task was completed. He claimed no worthiness in all that he purposed to do. He framed a prayer of touching tenderness, which he would use if he lived to see his father; and with this preparation he was ready to go from the scenes of his deep misery.

There was not an hour of procrastination with the prodigal. Is it not a wonder that he did not take some time to consider the length and danger of the journey, his own change of appearance and apparel, the expenses of the long travel, whether there might not be some of his former friends who would loan or give him enough to begin again in the world, how much his employer owed him, whether he could get another to take his place, and many other questions that might be considered? It is usual with sinners to hesitate a long time before they determine to be unreservedly on the Lord's side; and it is but seldom that their religious convictions are as deep as were those of this poor prodigal. The only easy and safe way to accomplish any work is to begin at once, and not to sit down dreading the undertaking. It is but seldom that a man purposes to be religious at a specified future time who keeps the resolution and begins at the time. We do not know an instance in the New Testament where any person planned in the morning of the day when he accepted Christ that he would accept him on that day. No part of the recital is more impressive than the account of the ease and success with which the prodigal returned home. "And he arose, and came to his father." To make his preparations for leaving home, his journey, his change of habits and life, his excesses and his beggary, require a painful recital of follies; but to return to the mercy and forgiveness of the father, the will and the deed seem to be simultaneous. Many a sinner is surprised to find how near he was to God, and how soon the Lord was found. He but stretched forth a withered hand, and it was made whole as the other. Still we must know that the prodigal's return home from a far country required time and cost labor and fatigue. Doubtless his anxiety and fear increased as he approached the object of his faith and trust. The adage, "The darkest hour is just before day," might be applied to him. How his heart would palpitate as he came near enough to recognize and remember familiar objects! A score of years have fled to eternity since he last saw them. He passes a man who was his neighbor, and he observes the effect of the stealthy tread of time on his frame, and remembers many incidents connected with this man, but the man knows not the prodigal. His bare feet, his rags, his sunken eye, his wasted frame, hide him from recognition by all except a father's love. God alone sees the first rising emotions of contrition in the soul of a penitent sinner. Yonder the prodigal beholds the old church where he often heard without heeding the gracious call of his Heavenly Father to repentance and faith in his Son. How he thinks of the dear familiar pew where the family sat in the long past, the well-worn Bible from which the preacher brought forth treasures new and old, the altar where his mother knelt and received the broken body and shed blood of her Redeemer whom she loved so well, and where the minister poured on his head the holy water of baptism! O how painful and yet how sweet are his memories! He crosses now the path made hard "by the feet that went up to the worship of God," and he begins to think of the faithful ones. Soon he passes the boundary line, and his foot rests upon his father's soil. Inheritance forfeited, and his heart fails. Anon from an eminence he descries the old homestead. When recovered from his emotions a little, he exclaims:

> As every prospect rises to my view,
> I seem to live departed years anew.

How tender and how dreadful the sight before him! He sees the very room where his mother knelt and prayed for him, asking unutterable blessings. There remains in the yard the stately elm under whose shade he had so often rested. Where is his father? He is so near home, and yet so full of alarm. Are all dead? Will any one receive me? I must advance.

> I can but perish if I go,
> I am resolved to try;
> For if I stay away I know
> I must forever die.

"But when he was yet a great way off, his father saw him, and had compassion, and ran, and fell on his neck, and kissed him." Eyes of mercy seeing him at a distance, bowels of mercy full of compassion, feet of mercy running to meet him, arms of mercy falling on his neck, and kisses of mercy removing all his sins in one generous forgiveness. So does God, by his preventing grace, run before the sinner, anticipating his desires and beholding his necessities, and out of his unwasting fullness supplying all. All this was done for the prodigal, as he stood in rags, hungry, feet bare, and not having uttered a word of his prayer. O the compassion of God, keeping mercy for thousands!

Read the account, and you will see that the prodigal began his prayer but could not reach its conclusion, being interrupted by the father's love and care in beginning to provide for his wants. The most trustworthy servants are called to his assistance, the best robe must be put on him, the fatted calf must be killed, a ring on his finger and shoes on his feet must be provided, and all the people called to the rejoicing; for this his son was dead and is alive again, he was lost and is found.

Lastly, the character of the self-righteous is portrayed.

There may be some praiseworthy qualities found in the elder brother; but we are not certain of it, f we look narrowly into his conduct. He resembles very much the self-righteous, who claim their abstaining from known sins and their prudence, which is for their own benefit, as their religion. The elder brother staid at home, but that may have been a selfish preference. All do not like to travel, and sometimes penuriousness prevents. A sinner may consider his own gain in his choice to follow home life.

In the beginning of the account we see that the elder brother was very ready to receive one-half of the goods on a division with his brother; but whether he ever contributed any labor or means to increase the estate, we do not know. It is true that he was out in the fields when his brother returned; but as the servants were all at the house, we presume that it was not the time for work in the fields. Probably he was idly strolling about the country. How many sinners, and some professing Christians, are eager to receive but slow to give! It would be a dangerous experiment for any government to offer all men pensions who would accept them, as bankruptcy would follow immediately; but it would be very safe to offer all the people a place to work without pay and from a principle of pure patriotism, as but few would accept the offer. The elder son's reflections that his father had not remembered him in killing a fatted calf and giving him a merrymaking time with his friends, shows how his mind was running in supreme selfishness on his own supplies. We have just read the statement of a preacher who professes to believe that baptism is for the remission of sins, that he would not baptize a person who avowed the intention to join another Church. In other words, he would allow a man to live with his sins upon him rather than see him unite with a Church that was opposed to his views. So this elder son would not willingly see his brother receive any favors unless he were included in the benefit; but he makes no offer to divide any part of the increase of the estate while his brother was away, and is not willing that his father shall contribute to the wants of the prodigal.

The censures of the elder brother fell upon the father as keenly and swiftly as they fell upon the wanderer. Men are ready to vindicate themselves at all times by denouncing the conduct of others, whether that conduct be good or bad. It is the easiest of all transfers to shift responsibility to the shoulders of another. Here, the elder brother was angry and displeased with all around him. His younger brother was an object of sympathy and compassion; his father blended parental authority with parental love, and the servants dutifully carried the messages of the father to the elder brother; but with indignation he scorned and spurned them all, and would not so much as go into the house. How often is it that sinners, in rejecting the message and the messengers of the Lord, complain of the Lord himself in the same breath! They receive all his benefits, and distrust all his providences and grace. They cannot understand why God has made them liable to sin and death. It seems to them that the close of life is soon enough to be religious, and that the prime of life should be devoted to business, or pleasure, or gain, or fame, or the gratification of all sinful lusts. Why religion should be an expensive thing is to them a standing mystery and subject of complaint. They cannot understand why the Churches should ever disagree, or why any of their members should show any imperfection, or why any duty in the Church should lie at their door, or why honesty and morality will not qualify them for heaven as well as the grace of God and the blood of Jesus. The last discovery that the self-righteous will ever make will be to ascertain that they are in fault. With many this discovery will only be made at the sitting of the great assizes. Even there they will say: "Lord, Lord, have we not prophesied in thy name, and in thy name done many wonderful works?" The curtain falls forever, and a voice is heard, saying: "I never knew you."

The Great Supper.

"And when one of them that sat at meat with him heard these things, he said unto him, Blessed is he that shall eat bread in the kingdom of God. Then said he unto him, A certain man made a great supper, and bade many; and sent his servant at supper-time to say to them that were bidden, Come; for all things are now ready. And they all with one consent began to make excuse. The first said unto him, I have bought a piece of ground, and I must needs go and see it; I pray thee have me excused. And another said, I have bought five yoke of oxen, and I go to prove them; I pray thee have me excused. And another said, I have married a wife, and therefore I cannot come. So that servant came, and showed his lord these things. Then the master of the house being angry said to his servant, Go out quickly into the streets and lanes of the city, and bring in hither the poor, and the maimed, and the halt, and the blind. And the servant said, Lord, it is done as thou hast commanded, and yet there is room. And the lord said unto the servant, Go out into the highways and hedges, and compel them to come in, that my house may be filled. For I say unto you, That none of those men which were bidden shall taste of my supper." Luke xiv. 15–24.

JESUS was in the house of one of the chief Pharisees, an invited guest to eat bread on the Sabbath-day. We are not to suppose that he desired a feast to be prepared for him, as we have no account that grand dinings and other feastings were arranged for our Lord, as are too common with his followers in the ministry, especially while protracted meetings are being held. One of the surest and most common means employed by Satan to forestall a revival in a protracted meeting is to pamper the appetite.

But this was a rare occasion, when even a Pharisee on the Sabbath-day had a grand feast, and invited guests of distinction, like the ladies at the President's levee, clamored for the first and best seats. Having secured the Lord's presence at a time and place of doubtful propriety, so far as the inviters and providers were concerned, they made it their chief business to watch him. Their motives and conduct were the same as would be displayed by a crowd of sinners on seeing a good man unexpectedly enter a theater or ball-room. But our Lord turned it all to good account.

Directly a man with the dropsy stood before Jesus. Categorically he asked the lawyers and Pharisees present, "Is it lawful to heal on the Sabbath-day?" It is very likely they had brought the sick man to the place as a special temptation. The lawyers and Pharisees held their peace, and did not answer the question. They intended to show a technical violation of the law if the man should be healed; and yet it was difficult to assert it in the presence

The Great Supper.

of the feast which they had prepared on the Sabbath-day. They must have had some impression that the Lord might heal the man, and to that extent they professed a faith for which they were responsible. It will be a great responsibility if all sinners are held accountable for all the faith that they possess. Before their eyes the Lord took the man and healed him, and let him go. He sanctified the house of sin by a work of charity. What an excellent example to those who are unexpectedly found on forbidden ground!

When the healing was done, our Lord entered upon a course of lessons to the lawyers and Pharisees. The first was to let them know that under certain circumstances of personal interest any one of them would do work on the Sabbath-day. If they should have an ass or an ox to fall into a pit, considering its value and the necessity for immediate relief, they would extricate it at once. Then passing from this technical violation of law, he proceeded to show them a far greater sin which they had on that day committed before his eyes. Each one had pressed forward, choosing for himself the chief rooms. He preferred himself to his neighbor, and did not wait for the owner of the house to assign him a place. He showed them that pride had sent them to the chief rooms, while humility dictated the lowest rooms on their entering the house. Then turning to the man who bid him to the feast, he showed his sin in a most unexpected light. Instead of inviting a company of rich neighbors and kinsmen to such a feast, true religion taught that he should have called the poor, the maimed, the lame, and the blind, who could not recompense him with another feast. At the conclusion of these unexpected lessons in the presence of a gay and proud company, one who was impressed with our Lord's teachings observed, "Blessed is he that shall eat bread in the kingdom of God." And this remark drew forth the parable that we are now to consider.

It is worthy of note that our Lord did not address the parable to the critical and fault-finding crowd, but to the person who made the remark just quoted. He was a hopeful hearer, while they were hopeless hearers. There is no profit in casting pearls before swine. From this let every minister take a judicious hint. It is often the case that some one or more of the sinners in the congregation should be addressed rather than the whole audience. The minister may easily show them by look and gesture that he is directing his remarks to them, and that he is in sympathy with their convictions.

The parable of the prodigal son and this parable begin with the same words—"A certain man." In that we considered the words as applied to God the Father, while here they apply to Jesus the Son

The Great Supper.

of the Father. There we behold the goodness of God in his general provisions for his family; here we have the work of the Lord our Saviour in all his rich furnishing of gospel means and grace. Let us consider his labor of love.

A certain man made a great supper. "Feed my sheep, feed my lambs," said the Master. With the Jews the supper was the chief meal; with all, the bread furnished by our Lord is the ample and only provision for the soul in time and in eternity. Look at the large supply.

In one sacrament Jesus gave his own body, broken for us, and his own blood shed for us. Earth has no supply that can offer a comparison. What an immense change if the man who made the feast on the Sabbath-day had not only supplied his guests with all pleasant and nutritious food, but had also given himself to relieve them from some dreadful debt or penalty! This our Redeemer has done. He said of himself: "I am the bread of life; he that cometh to me shall never hunger, and he that believeth on me shall never thirst." He said again: "Except ye eat the flesh of the Son of man, and drink his blood, ye have no life in you. Whoso eateth my flesh, and drinketh my blood, hath eternal life; and I will raise him up at the last day. For my flesh is meat indeed, and my blood is drink indeed. He that eateth my flesh, and drinketh my blood, dwelleth in me, and I in him." This is that bread which came down from heaven. Hear the Master once more: "And as they were eating, Jesus took bread, and blessed it, and brake it, and gave it to the disciples, and said, Take, eat; this is my body. And he took the cup, and gave thanks, and gave it to them, saying, Drink ye all of it; for this is my blood of the new testament, which is shed for many for the remission of sins." Read the Apostle Paul on the same subject: "For I have received of the Lord that which also I delivered unto you, That the Lord Jesus, the same night in which he was betrayed, took bread; and when he had given thanks, he brake it, and said, Take, eat; this is my body, which is broken for you; this do in remembrance of me. After the same manner also he took the cup, when he had supped, saying, This cup is the new testament in my blood; this do ye, as oft as ye drink it, in remembrance of me. For as often as ye eat this bread, and drink this cup, ye do show the Lord's death till he come." Here is a feast, indeed, in which the Giver has given himself for us. The whole humanity of Jesus Christ is given for man alone. Mark the emphasis with which he declares that the cup is the new testament in his blood. Every line of the Scriptures and every provision of grace have their only merit in the blood of Jesus Christ; and without the shedding of blood there is no remission of sins. .

But much more than himself is given by our Lord in the Great Supper. He has given his word to be a lamp to our feet, and a light to our path. He has given his Church, in which there are many nursing fathers and mothers for the young and the weak. He teaches us to pray, "Give us this day our daily bread," and a rich supply is sent as surely as manna fell in the wilderness. He has given his ministers a command to preach the unsearchable riches of Christ, and to feed the flock over which the Holy Ghost hath made them overseers.

See how his kindness is enlarged beyond the bountiful supper which the Lord hath prepared.

First, he bid many to the supper. He was heard saying: "Come unto me, all ye ends of the earth, and be ye saved. Come unto me, all ye that labor and are heavy-laden, and I will give you rest." In shedding his blood and giving his broken body for us, as already named, he tasted death for every man; he became absolutely no respecter of persons. It was intended to be a large affair, where love should be manifested to all, and where none could complain of any lack in the supply. He gave time for all to prepare and come to the supper, from the day of the first invitation to the day when the feast was ready. Every sinner reading these pages has had as much time for repentance as is necessary to do any work of life; and each day he has lived under the authoritative command of God to prepare to-day, and not to wait for the morrow. Warnings on the one hand and promises on the other have made a wall of motives as high as heaven to induce a hearty and ready compliance with the invitation. The acceptance of this feast has been the prescribed duty of life, and its rejection the dangerous sin of life. With all these considerations before him, each man lives every day in the sight of God.

The double invitation extended to the invited shows the large-heartedness of our Lord, and increases the guilt of the rejecters. In a general way on the first day he bid many, and then on the day and at the hour when all the preparations were complete he sent his servant at supper-time to give another invitation, supposing that some might forget the hour. Men would be responsible for their souls if salvation were offered only through the Scriptures; but lest these should not be heeded, God sends his servants at the very hour when he waits to be gracious—sometimes the minister with the preached word, then the Christian in prayers offered for the sinner, or in relating his own experience, and by the example of his religious life calling the attention of every one to the value of the feast and the danger of delay. A court of justice will send only one peremptory summons to a party commanding a certain thing to be done months hence and on a specified day, and this is sufficient

THE GREAT SUPPER. 133

in law to compel compliance; but the court of heaven gives line upon line, and at the last and most opportune moment, while the gate of mercy is open wide, sends a special invitation to the guilty to escape for their life, and enjoy the rich repast furnished by their Lord.

No less remarkable and gracious are the words employed in the last invitation—"Come, for all things are now ready." The possibility is implied in the invitation that in the universe of God there may be one not ready, and that one may be the invited. Ten thousand beings are in sight—some in heaven, and some in hell—who have no personal interest in the invitation, but they are all ready. Can it be possible that the invited, the favored, the called, the redeemed, the beneficiaries of the feast for time and for eternity, may not be ready to accept the gracious invitation? Yes, it is not only possible, but painfully true. Here is matter of amazement for three worlds. Every devil in hell is ready to oppose the return of the soul to Jesus. Every angel in heaven is ready to aid in the return, and to show joy in heaven the instant it takes place. Every saint, living or dead, is ready to aid in the good work of accepting Christ. Every intercession of the Lord himself shows that he is the ready Advocate with the Father. Every suggestion of enlightened reason on the part of the invited urges to instant readiness in accepting the invitation. Every emotion of conscience pleads against a rejection of Christ; and yet the invited often refuse, procrastinate, and may be lost.

The treatment of the invitation by the party named is here stated as the treatment of all the invited who reject Christ, and it stands forth remarkable as being a total failure. Even the man who said, "Blessed is he that shall eat bread in the kingdom of God," and to whom the Lord is speaking, has gone no farther toward accepting Christ. What intolerably hardened sinners the lawyers and Pharisees then present must have been who had broken their own law on the Sabbath-day, hoping that Jesus would do the same thing, and all of whom maintained a silent rejection of Christ! Once in the life of our Lord, certain men besought him to depart out of their coasts, and he did so, and so far as the history goes he never returned to them.

Here three of the invited, representing the whole class of rejecters, with one consent began to make excuse as soon as they heard the last and kindest invitation. No doubt between the first and the last invitation they had at various conferences agreed upon a certain line of conduct in the way of opposition, just as sinners do every day. It is remarkable how men having the most conflicting interests can agree in opposing religion. Herod and Pilate would probably have never made friends if it had not been for their joint purpose to destroy Jesus. No doubt these men were but seldom together, and would not have been on that day if it had not been for their anxiety to strengthen each other in their opposition to the supper. One was a land-buyer, adding farm to farm; another was a man actively engaged in business, buying oxen and proving them to see if they would work well; while the third was a man of domestic ease and indolence. Such variety of employment and disposition proves that they were not intimate associates. Their reasons for not attending the supper are very different, yet each can see in the other's excuse a sufficient justification. So it is with sinners. Any word spoken or act done against the Church and the religion of Christ is at once received by every one with approval. The heart is deceitful above all things, and desperately wicked.

Observe there is no delay on the part of either of the three in preferring their excuse. The devil does not allow sinners to parley with the question of accepting or rejecting Christ. He knows that truth, reason, conscience, interest, and safety are all on the side of instant obedience. So by masterly strategy he avoids procrastination, and induces the foolish and unwary to refuse outright to have the man Christ Jesus to reign over them. If they were allowed sufficient time to look at the consequences, and ask whether there be any other name given under heaven among men whereby salvation was possible, they might fly to the Redeemer. But on the other hand, Satan persuades all who are inclined to be religious to pause and take time, and weigh their own unworthiness, and wait until they feel good enough for the Church, and be very certain that they are converted and have sufficient strength never to fall from grace. In the same moment Satan whispers, "Follow me at once, but do not follow Christ until many days hence."

Our Lord teaches all men an important lesson in the example of the three rejecters in the parable. Each one gave a reason that was true in itself, but the question was one of *sufficiency* in the sight of God, and not of bare truth in the statement. A thousand true statements may be made as excuses for being irreligious, but until one is found that will satisfy the Lord, all are insufficient before the Judge. Here it was true that one of the men had bought a piece of ground, and another had bought five yoke of oxen, and another had married a wife, but none of these were good reasons for not attending the supper. In the first two instances the trades were made, and the examination could be postponed a day; and in the last instance the man had married a wife, and he was secure in his possession. On the very face of the excuses no good reason was given for failing to go to the supper; and so it is with all excuses of all sinners.

The sinner says that he would be religious if all

the Churches were agreed on the teachings of the Bible; but he has joined some political party without waiting for an agreement among politicians—indeed, their disagreement increases his partisan zeal. He employs a physician when he is sick, knowing that all the schools of medicine disagree. He goes to law with his neighbor, and contends for his supposed rights, while the subject is necessarily one of disagreement. He enters a store and buys goods for his family, without being certain that he is securing the best fabrics. If all Christians were agreed on all questions, infidelity and the devil would allege that very fact as proof of collusion. One alarming feature to the sinner on this subject is that all the Churches, even while in a state of disagreement, hold that he is wrong and in imminent danger. Twelve witnesses in court agreeing to a fact, when it is known that they are enemies on other subjects, give more convincing testimony than twelve who were friends, and may have concerted together to give the same account.

The sinner says that religion is a very serious matter, and he should take time and be deliberate. Yes, it is true that religion is a very serious matter; but is that a just reason on the part of the sinner to take time throughout life, thinking and following other pursuits, and banishing all thoughts of his own salvation from his mind? His own confession proves his sense of responsibility. He does not ask the same time on any other subject, but at once proceeds to act on the best light that he has before him. We give only two as specimens of all the excuses made by sinners.

Thus we see that nearly all excuses of sinners for being irreligious are true in the statement made, but not one is a sufficient justification in the light of reason or according to the command of the word of God. The man who said to Jesus, "Lord, suffer me first to go and bury my father," had apparently the best excuse in the Bible. Whether his father was then dead and awaiting sepulture, or whether he was far advanced in the decline of life and required the attention of the son, the result was the same. The command, "To-day if ye will hear his voice, harden not your hearts," was of paramount obligation. If the call of the man was to the ministry, it was of supreme moment. Confessing the Lord before men was not in the way of any duty. When Elisha was plowing in the field, and Elijah passed by and cast his mantle upon him, thereby calling him to special service, and he lovingly asked Elijah to allow him to go and kiss his father and mother before he left home, promising obedience immediately after his return, he was not allowed time to turn out of the way for that purpose. What then shall be said of the large numbers who Gallio-like care for none of these things, or who with contemptuous scorn and indifference make light of all religious duty? Truly they will find that it is a fearful thing to fall into the hands of the living God!

The doctrine taught in this parable is that the provisions of the gospel are large, free, and intended for all men.

The thought originates in the selfishness of the human heart, and in the knowledge that among men there is always respect of persons, that God has favorites among mankind, and that he does not intend to fill even the righteous with plenty. From Adam to Christ, and from Christ to the nineteenth century, every dispensation and each generation show an enlargement of the mercy and grace of God. No such thing appears in any age of the Church as a withdrawal of powers or opportunities given at a former period. In every turn of the wheels of time the light from heaven is increased, and with the light more grace and mercy are added. In olden times God spoke face to face to the few, and the few gave the knowledge thus received to the many; but in this day, by his Son and through his word, he gives the knowledge of present and eternal salvation to all men. Many who were supposed from their writings to hold the doctrine of personal election and reprobation from eternity are now employing their best strength in asserting that their books never taught the horrible doctrines attributed to them.

We live in a period of all others the most auspicious. By long observation and experience covering nearly twenty centuries, it is manifest to all thinking men that the Church triumphs, whether in apparent weakness or in evident strength. There is a demonstration in all lands that reaches the door of the hearts of the ungodly that the Christian religion is no cunningly devised fable, but that it is the truth of God. Not one man in a thousand finds any thing in this world, apart from the atonement of Christ, which he seeks as his dying comfort. Perhaps no thought is of such universal acceptance in Christendom to-day as the belief that Christ died for all men. Looking into every city, town, and place, the devil can use only the riffraff of the population. Approaching each one the spires of the churches pointing toward heaven are the objects seen at the greatest distance and the first to attract the eye. Entering any cemetery, no names are mentioned but Christ and the saints who have died. Only a quarter of a century ago our missionary, the Rev. Charles Taylor, was the first to enter Soochow, China, and he went in disguise; but now the gospel is freely preached in that heathen city, and colleges and schools are opened in the land. What hath God wrought! The fields are white unto the harvest. If we who live now could live here a century longer, we should behold all the world ablaze with the glory of Christ.

As it is true that Jesus tasted death for all men, so it is true that he provides for all a royal and abundant feast. His gospel is as free as the air that we breathe. His grace that bringeth salvation hath appeared to all men, and is richer than the gold of Ophir. Well may we sing:

> Enough for all, enough for each,
> Enough for evermore.

The duty taught in the parable is instant obedience to the commands of Christ, connected with increased responsibility for disobedience.

Looking at nature, we see the heavens declaring the glory of God and the firmanent showing his handiwork. If we reason on the subject, we hear a voice saying: "Come now, and let us reason together; though your sins be as scarlet, they shall be as white as snow." In our depraved hearts we are oppressed with the thought, "When we would do good, evil is present with us." From our Lord the words reach us: "Come unto me; I will give you rest." There is laid before our eyes and at the door of our hearts the assurance that his blood cleanseth from all sin. To insure prompt action, we read: "Boast not thyself of to-morrow; to-day is the accepted time." Our winged flight is such that a single day makes the distance less to eternity. We are startled by the appealing cry from heaven, "Why will ye die?" Seeking for light and strength in a crooked and perverse world, we soon ascertain that there is no other name than the name of Jesus given under heaven among men for salvation; and yet with one consent not only three, but ten thousand, make excuse. O how fearful their doom if they continue longer in rebellion! O the joy in heaven if they now accept Christ! Will the reader be one of the ten thousand, or will he exclaim:

>I yield, I yield,
>I can hold out no more;
>I sink by dying love compelled,
>And own thee conqueror?

The Good Samaritan.

"And, behold, a certain lawyer stood up, and tempted him, saying, Master, what shall I do to inherit eternal life? He said unto him, What is written in the law? how readest thou? And he answering said, Thou shalt love the Lord thy God with all thy heart, and with all thy soul, and with all thy strength, and with all thy mind; and thy neighbor as thyself. And he said unto him, Thou hast answered right; this do, and thou shalt live. But he, willing to justify himself, said unto Jesus, And who is my neighbor? And Jesus answering said, A certain man went down from Jerusalem to Jericho, and fell among thieves, which stripped him of his raiment, and wounded him, and departed, leaving him half dead. And by chance there came down a certain priest that way; and when he saw him, he passed by on the other side. And likewise a Levite, when he was at the place, came and looked on him, and passed by on the other side. But a certain Samaritan, as he journeyed, came where he was; and when he saw him, he had compassion on him. And went to him, and bound up his wounds, pouring in oil and wine, and set him on his own beast, and brought him to an inn, and took care of him. And on the morrow when he departed, he took out two pence, and gave them to the host, and said unto him, Take care of him; and whatsoever thou spendest more, when I come again, I will repay thee. Which now of these three, thinkest thou, was neighbor unto him that fell among the thieves? And he said, He that showed mercy on him.

Then said Jesus unto him, Go, and do thou likewise." St. Luke x. 25–37.

A MEAN principle is sometimes the occasion of a striking parable of our Lord. He was so condescending to the wants of men that he would not allow such motives as appeared in this instance to deter him from delivering valuable truth. A certain lawyer stood up and tempted the Lord, asking him, "Master, what shall I do to inherit eternal life?" As he was a lawyer, he was probably very adroit in presenting difficult and entangling questions; and such we presume was his motive here, which is one far from being commendable. The adroitness of the question is seen in its apparently innocent inquiry concerning his own duty, and yet capable of being construed when answered—as attacking the doctrine of grace if answered in one way, or the duty of good works if answered in another. In his frame of mind it would have availed nothing to draw distinctions between controverted differences among theologians. He being a lawyer, Christ referred him to his own law, and obliged him to answer. That law went far beyond all human codes; it originated in grace, and was completed in good works. The law commanded us to love God with all the heart, soul, mind, and strength, and our neighbor as ourself. But few were spiritual enough for the first requirement, and the last was almost forgotten in the midst of universal selfishness. When he had truly declared the law, Jesus said to him, "This do, and thou shalt live." Not having done either, and especially the latter, and the lawyer being willing to justify himself—which is perhaps the first and most universal impulse with every man—raised the only question that gave him a hope of escape, asking, "Who is my neighbor?" Is it the man living on an adjoining farm? Is it the one who lives next door to me on the street? Is it those who belong to my party or my religion? Is it my friend or my kindred? Surely it is not my enemy. This question, "Who is my neighbor?" brought forth the parable before us.

In the figures employed in this parable we have a most important lesson taught that may be overlooked. The poor sufferer who fell among thieves was found *going the wrong way*. Perhaps it was not intentional on his part to go the wrong way; but ruin will follow as certainly by a travel on the wrong road as if the worst designs were harbored in the soul. "A certain man went down from Jerusalem to Jericho." He was found going *down* to Jericho; he was not found going *up* to Jerusalem. From every direction those who went to Jerusalem were said to go up to Jerusalem, while those who went to Jericho went down to Jericho. Jerusalem was the city of the great king. Jerusalem above is the mother of us all. We sing:

> Jerusalem, my happy home,
> Name ever dear to me.

Jerusalem stood much higher than Jericho—the latter being six hundred feet lower than the Mediterranean Sea. As the traveler approached Jericho he found a desolate and rocky region, fit for thieves and robbers, described in the Book of Joshua as "the wilderness that goeth up from Jericho."

Jerusalem was the favorite of God. Here his people dwelt, and here was his temple, the house of prayer. Jerusalem was full of light. It was the city of peace. The very name sounds sweetly. Jericho was a profane city, and under a curse. In Joshua we read: "Cursed be the man before the Lord, that riseth up and buildeth this city Jericho." The evil day in the life of Lot was when Abraham, giving him choice to possess the right-hand of the country, which seemed hilly and unfruitful at first sight, or the left-hand, which was level and rich and well watered at the beginning, chose the left, and *pitched his tent toward Sodom*. Every night when he paused and pitched his tent toward Sodom, he was nearer the sinful and doomed city than he had been in the morning. Every step that the man took toward Jericho carried him farther from Jerusalem, where there was safety and peace, and nearer to Jericho, which was resting under the curse of God. Let us apply this thought. When Dr. Franklin was a boy, and his friends filled his pockets with pennies and he went forth to enjoy the holiday, he found a boy with a whistle. At once he offered him all his money for the whistle; but when his friends told him how much more he had paid for the whistle than it was worth, and how many other things he could have bought with his money, he was filled with shame and grief. He remembered it in all his after life; and when he found a young man for very little consideration going into sin, he was accustomed to say, "He is paying too dear for the whistle." When Esau desired a mess of pottage so much that he gave his birthright for it, he was purchasing a heavy load of repentance.

There is not an eminence so high in all the world that a single step is not hazardous if taken in the downward direction of sin. The apostolic injunction, "Abstain from all appearance of evil," is not too strong, and is full of prudence and good sense. Every young man who thinks he can sow his wild oats and leave off at pleasure is acting as foolishly and rashly as one who plays with fire near a magazine of gunpowder.

Place and associates have much to do with human safety and happiness. What strength it would have been to Lot if ten righteous persons had been found in Sodom! But he stood alone; and the effect of evil associations is seen in his course as soon as he escaped from danger. The family, and particularly his daughters, did not fail to take a supply of wine with them when they left the city, but the religious virtues of Abraham they had lost. With the wine Lot was soon and easily made drunk. We can almost see he is keeping up the evil practices in which he had probably indulged in Sodom. Any one sin allowed by a Christian will be more clamorous for indulgence the oftener it is repeated.

The priest who passed by on the other side when he saw the unfortunate man who had fallen among thieves is supposed to have been a citizen of Jericho. This place was said to have been head-quarters for the priests. Here, away from Jerusalem, they could indulge forbidden pleasures, and so it became a motto, "Like priest, like people." Coming from a place so wicked as Jericho, it was not strange that he had lost the feeling of common humanity for a sufferer. Every evil association and practice in Jericho would harden his heart. His priestly robes were not thick enough to keep out the devil. His example was contagious to the Levite. He would say: "If the priest refuses to help the poor man, I may do the same thing." Exactly the same words are used as to the two: "They saw the man, and passed by on the other side"—the Levite following in the very tracks of the priest. It was the office of the Levites to attend the priests in their duties. So we see that travel to Jericho is much more dangerous than travel to Jerusalem, and that Jericho is a dangerous abode for the priest or the people. As a Christian passes a theater, or a ball-room, or a saloon, he should hold his breath until he escapes; but if he is passing a church, he may sing praises to God. To abide in the evil places just named is to venture near the brink of the bottomless pit.

Jericho was twenty-one miles from Jerusalem. This distance is far too great for a sinner to take in his own strength. He will fall among thieves before the journey is done. Jericho was once called the city of palm-trees, but now it is a miserable village of only a few houses. Sin has shorn it of its glory. Jericho was the first city taken by Joshua fourteen hundred and fifty years before Christ, and it fell by the will of God through the blowing of rams' horns. Its beautiful name—the city of palm-trees—and its great age do no not save it from sin and the just judgments of God for its wickedness. Its history is the history of sin in an individual life—beginning in the morning like a city of palm-trees, closing in the evening in poverty and filth and shame.

The priest and Levite in the parable represent formal professors of religion, who are destitute of true godliness. Their religious profession makes their crime the greater and more evident than if they were common sinners. In the Mosaic law, under which the priest was commissioned to act, the spirit of kindness to strangers and enemies was taught: "If thou meet thine enemy's ox or his ass going astray, thou shalt surely bring it back to him again. If thou see the ass of him that hateth thee lying under his burden, and wouldest forbear to help him, thou shalt surely help with him." (Ex. xxiii. 4, 5.) So the two were left without excuse. It is supposed that the priest framed as an excuse for his want of humanity that he was in haste to get to Jerusalem to enter upon his course of service in the temple; but how much fairer would his character have shone before his peers if, entering Jerusalem a day after the beginning of his term, he had said: "I was detained by hearing the groans of a man almost dead whom I found along the way, and stopped to bind up his wounds."

> O how can they look up to heaven,
> And ask for mercy there,
> Who never soothed the poor man's pang,
> Nor dried the orphan's tear?

The sin of the priest was increased by the fact that the sufferer was a Jew, and one of his own blood. While we are to love our enemies and do good to all men, yet certain relations of life increase our obligations to certain people. Our own children justly receive more of our care than the children of our neighbors; the true husband will love his own wife as he loves himself; the true wife will regard her own husband more tenderly than she regards all other men; the true minister cares for the flock of his own feeding more than he cares for another. A Jewish priest should have cared for a suffering Jew. But his guilt will burn in his bones as long as it is known that he left him in the hands of a stranger, and one whose nation was an enemy of his own, and in a place of great danger, while the sufferer was wounded almost to death.

In considering the conduct of the Samaritan, we reach the important doctrine of the text—"Do unto others as you would have them do unto you." Do good unto all men.

The Samaritan may be supposed to have national and personal antipathy to the wounded Jew. Often the former begets the latter, and the two increase the hatred. In war, in heated political contests, and sometimes in religious differences, the antipathy of all the people on either side to the other is transferred to the individuals, and is full of rancor. The Jews and Samaritans were enemies politically and religiously. Theirs was no common or ordinary hate. To increase the likelihood of this feeling on the part of this Samaritan, he may have perceived that the priest and Levite left the wounded man to die, and might naturally conclude from their conduct that he was either some criminal who deserved death or some worthless character who was outside the pale of worldly humanity. What a noble character he must have possessed to be moved by none of these considerations to pass by the wretched man, but forgetting every thing except that *he was a man in great distress*, stopped to relieve him! The late war furnished many noble examples on both sides of men who forgot the strife in an hour of personal distress, and stooped to succor those whom the authorities called mortal enemies. A cup of cold water given by a soldier to his sick and dying enemy will be remembered in heaven when every note of the trump of earthly fame has ceased forever.

As well as the priest and Levite, the Samaritan might have pleaded the prior claims of the business which called him to that section, or he might have considered that his time was too valuable to be lost for one whom he did not know; or he might have said: "The thieves have taken all that the man possessed, and it is impossible that he should compensate me for my trouble and expenses;" or he might have feared, when he saw how badly the man was wounded, that if he once undertook to be his friend days or weeks would pass before he could give up attention and be free from responsibility; or he might have concluded that the state of his own purse was inadequate to the present and future demands that would be upon it; or he might have feared that the thieves were lurking around, and would overtake him and treat him as they had treated the wounded man; or he might have determined, as the wounded man was his national en-

The Good Samaritan. 153

emy, to pass on, trusting that some Jews kinder than the priest and Levite would come to his help. What a noble man he must have been to be moved by none of these suggestions of selfishness! He was the Good Samaritan indeed. He resembles the Good Shepherd who cares for the sheep, and who went after one that was lost in a flock of a hundred, leaving the ninety and nine, never resting until he found it, and then carrying it home on his own shoulders many weary miles. Would the writer and the reader have done as the Good Samaritan did on that day?

Let us examine his labor of love.

He had *compassion* on the wounded man. Here is the test of true religion. Compassion was the secret spring of his actions. Whoever is born of God feels for the suffering. If a man love not his brother whom he hath seen, how can he love God whom he hath not seen? Jesus so estimates good works in the way of kindness to others as to regard them as being done to himself. Selfishness asks, "How can a man love the millions of idolaters in China whom he has never seen?" The answer is because Christ died for every soul in China, and each one who has felt the redeeming blood of the Lord in his own soul will have a strong sympathy for all peoples embraced in the atonement.

Every thing that the Samaritan did was done in

the right *order of time*. He did not first carry the sufferer to the inn, and contract shrewdly with the inn-keeper for food, medicines, and attention, and then when a good bargain was made begin the work of relief, but instantly that he had compassion he began with all the means in his power to assuage his pains. Here is a lesson of great value. We are not to wait before we preach Christ to the dying until we are educated, and having a large experience, and gifts of cultivated oratory, and a loud money-call; but as the soul is needy now, we are now to proclaim its redemption. We are not to postpone religious instruction to our children until they are of ripe years and mature understanding, as by that time Satan will possess head and heart. We are not to withhold a loaf of bread from the poor until our barns are full and running over, for they may sooner than that event starve to death. We may not refuse to send the gospel to the heathen as long as there are heathen at home, for this will be true until the millennium.

Behold the *number* and *kind* of benefactions of the Samaritan. With his own hands, by the wayside, and before he knew his name, he bound up the wounds of the poor man; then from his own supply he poured in oil and wine to mollify the intense suffering; by his own strength he sat him on his own beast, and took the journey afoot. How many miles he thus carried him we do not know;

but he did not leave him for a moment until he reached a public inn, where he could purchase supplies and help. When he reached the inn, not regarding his own fatigue, he watched him during the night, and did not rely upon careless nurses. On the morrow, when the sick man was sufficiently relieved to be left, he gave his own money to the host, and engaged him to take care of the man. He went farther, and assured the host that whatsoever he spent on the man he would pay on his return. He did not limit the inn-keeper as to the amount that he should expend on his credit. He did not exact from the sufferer a promise that he would repay him when he recovered and was able to repay. The bare statement of his good deeds virtually answered the question that was ready to be propounded: "Which of the three—priest, Levite or Samaritan—was neighbor to the poor man?"

Spasmodic works of goodness find but little favor with God or with men. Reliability is one of the best qualities of every performance. The man who said, "I go, sir," and went not, received no reward. "Whatsoever thy hand findeth to do, do it with thy might," and continue in the work. A life is symmetrical when it is all alike—never ceasing from good works, and never periodically excited by the occasion. Sunday Christians who are Monday cheats are too numerous. Too many persons join in good deeds, if many are engaged in the same work, at the same time, and when the performance is conspicuous. The Good Samaritan worked alone, but his heart and his hands were willing. Very many Christians require urging and entreating all the time to do their duty. Every Church is compelled to have officers to collect money, and see that specific duties are performed. Probably not one-half of the members of any congregation would ever voluntarily discharge their plain duty if no appeal were made to them. Every Christian should make every man's necessities his own, and see that his own face is all the time toward Jerusalem.

The bitten Israelites looked toward the brazen serpent to be healed, and not in an opposite direction. When Solomon dedicated the temple, he knelt down and prayed, spreading forth his hands toward heaven for help, and not toward the earth. His petition was that prayers offered in that house, as well as those offered toward that house, should be heard and answered from heaven. "Look unto me, and be ye saved," is the direction. Do not look away from the Lord expecting life. Each step that the prodigal took on his return was toward home, and not in the direction of a strange land. It gives the life of a man fixedness of purpose when every act is performed looking to Jesus. The rope-walker must have a balancing-pole and a single object on which he looks, or he will fall. The soldier is animated by certain national emblems and songs which he distinguishes from all others.

> The Christian lives to Christ alone,
> To Christ alone he dies.

"No man liveth unto himself," is the first and highest motive of human conduct. What a narrow circle if a man could do no good beyond himself! The food that he ate and the clothes that he wore would be the beginning and the end. How like a beast! Jesus went about doing good. This so distinguished him from others that it was noted in the Gospels as his peculiarity. We should be a peculiar people, zealous of good works. To do good and to communicate forget not, for with such sacrifices God is well pleased. The Good Samaritan was a neighbor to the man who fell among thieves, while the priest and Levite were strangers and enemies.

The deeds of the Good Samaritan are given in detail by our Lord as being the every-day work of the average Christian. They are not to be read and studied as a great and universal Church affair, happening once a year and performed only by remarkably eminent Christians, but such as belong to the work of each one in the Church on any day of the year. Can we bear an inspection of our hearts and lives in this comparison?

GOOD WORKS.

"Ye see then how that by works a man is justified, and not by faith only." James ii. 24.

JAMES means to be understood as saying there is a proper sense in which a man is justified by works and not by faith only. The word "how" in the text he emphasizes for this purpose. He is not by any means antagonizing the position that at the moment when we are born again we are justified by faith and have peace with God. His epistle is concerning the duties of the Christian life, and not the agency or power by which we enter upon that life. So far as he names faith it is to show the absurdity of supposing that a man can discharge all the duties of the Christian life by it, without any good works of obedience, simply because faith first led him to Christ. He was opposing the views of those who supposed that God did all our works for us and in us, and appointing certain persons from eternity to heirship with his Son; and, secondly, treating them as passive beings, to work as he gives the power. These views will be clearly seen to be correct, if we notice some of his illustrations.

To all Christians he shows that pure and undefiled religion consists of visiting the fatherless and widows in their affliction. It is not the enjoyment of a quiet faith at home while others are destitute of daily food. Its daily employment is found in good works. It is not so environed with the sovereignty of God that the Christian may go safely abroad without danger of falling while he neglects to keep himself "unspotted from the world." He is urging all to good works of active charity by warning Christians that a very vain religion will follow an unbridled tongue, although the words spoken may be supposed to be true and in vindication of the truth, as the heart will be deceived by such licentiousness. His condemnation of faith is not that kind which trusts Christ for life, and then lives to do his will on earth as it is done in heaven; but it is that faith which, in the name of Christ, has respect of persons. He condemns that worldly faith which welcomes to the best seat in the congregation the man who has a gold ring, but says to the poor man in vile raiment, "Sit under my footstool;" and all this without any reference to their true moral character. With such the rich man had the good seat at Church, while Lazarus remained at the door with the dogs. He was appealing to Christians to have a faith that would be shown by their works.

The position of James is made clear by his reference to Abraham. Possibly it was a score of years after Abraham had believed on God, according to Paul and James, and his faith was imputed to him for righteousness; and in all these years he had worked as God commanded, to prove his faith. A notable instance is given in these words: "Was not Abraham our father justified by works, when he had offered Isaac his son upon the altar? Seest thou how faith wrought with his works, and by works was faith made perfect? And the scripture was fulfilled which saith, Abraham believed God, and it was imputed unto him for righteousness; and he was called the Friend of God." So, then, James is affirming that a genuine faith as long as it continues will always be known by good works, faith and works each proving the other, and each indispensable in its place.

Paul uses the term "justified" in relation to faith, and James uses the same term in relation to works. The term, rightly understood, is appropriate to faith and works. Paul is speaking of the hour when the sinner first finds acceptance with God; and in that hour of supreme importance to him nothing but faith in Christ is realized, and it is true that the saved one is "justified by faith without the deeds of the law." James is speaking of the evil of resting upon faith after conversion without good works following; and in that view he can truly say: "Ye see then *how* that by works a man is justified, and not by faith only." The term "justified" is a law term, and like many law terms has more than one meaning, and is to be understood by its contextual relation.

We always have to approach good works cautiously; for while the Bible is full of them as our daily duty, yet the world is full of error; and just here we find the Antinomian view discarding works as of any moment with God who has commanded them, and the Pelagian view discarding grace and attributing all merit and ability to our own performances. Keeping in mind that faith in Christ is the only thing required of us to secure remission of sins, and that good works, without merit attached as a reward, are the constant proof that saving faith rests in the soul, we shall make no mistake when we give in detail the place that good works hold in the Christian system. Our Articles of Religion accord with the Scriptures in the following clear view of good works: "Although good works, which are the fruits of faith and follow after justification, cannot put away our sins, and endure the severity of God's judgment, yet are they pleasing and acceptable to God in Christ, and spring out of a true and lively faith, insomuch that by them a lively faith may be as evidently known as a tree is discerned by its fruit."

The command to work is as extensive and as imperative as the command to pray or to believe on Christ. When the Master said, "Son, go work to-day in my vineyard," and one who was commanded answered, "I will not, and afterward repented and went;" and when he issued the same command to another, who said, "I go, sir, and went not"—it was found that neither the declaration nor their performance affected or changed in the slightest degree the command to labor that was given to both in the same hour of the day. Running along with the command, "Remember the Sabbath-day, to keep it holy," is the equally urgent command, "Six days shalt thou labor." The garden of Eden was not left until sinning man was commanded to labor in tilling the ground. Four thousand years afterward an apostle addresses Christians, urging them not to be slothful in business, but to be diligent. Work seems to be the chief employment of earth; without it there is neither excellence nor reward. Solomon said: "Seest thou a man diligent in his business? he shall stand before kings." It would be singular if the Church and the religious life should be exempt from the universal provision of labor for all that is good.

There is no condition of life exempt from the obligation to do good works. Purity of soul does not create such exemption. Jesus was pure by nature and by grace inherently and as our representative; and yet he declared of himself: "For the works which the Father hath given me to finish, the same works that I do, bear witness of me, that the Father hath sent me." Afterward he declared to the Jews, "The works that I do in my Father's name, they bear witness of me." Toward the close of his precious life, he said to his Father: "I have finished the work which thou gavest me to do." Our Lord claimed his works as the proof of his faithfulness. Every day he went about doing good. He performed works of mercy, and not works of ostentation. The disciple is not above his Master. Shall we sit with folded hands, being all the day idle, and crying, "A little more sleep, and a little more slumber?" Let us arise and build. Paul's triumphant words in the view of approaching death were: "I have finished my course."

Works are commanded by the Master in proportion to every man's ability: "And unto one he gave five talents, to another two, and to another one; to every man according to his several ability." What a merciful kindness! If he had given but one talent to the servant who could use five, then four-fifths of his time and ability would have remained idle. If he had given five talents or even two talents to the man who could only use one, he would have been crushed under the exaction. But the order of Heaven is: "Require of each no more than he is able to do." This evident justice and mercy on the part of God will increase the responsibility of each one to do all that is commanded. If he shall lose a day he will never regain it, as every day has full work of its own. "Sufficient unto the day is the evil thereof." The good Samaritan is a well-drawn picture of good works to be performed by every Christian. First he had compassion on the poor man who fell among thieves, then he bound up his wounds, then he mollified them with oil and wine, then by his own strength he placed him on his own beast, then he carried him to an inn, then he nursed him all night, then he paid the host money for him, and then he left the landlord to expend more for the man without limit, and all without any demand or promise of repayment at any time.

Our works as Christians are prescribed oftener for others than for ourself. The labor with ourself is to persuade to a hearty and personal acceptance of Christ. But as to others the labor is to persuade us to love our neighbor as ourself. We will not forget our own wants, but we may forget those of another. Hence the Bible is full of directions to work for others. We are to prefer the honor of another to our own. If two complete the same enterprise, let each give the other the credit. Small deeds are more numerous and valuable than great ones. A cup of cold water given in the right name and with the right motive will not lose its reward. Every day we are to pray for all men—for kings and for all in authority, for the widow, the orphan, and the poor, for our enemies, and for all who despitefully use us. We may get along by giving the Lord one-tenth of our money, but he demands the homage of heart and life all the time. We are constantly to do good to all men, especially to the household of faith.

No good work is done in our own strength. The Holy Spirit is the efficient power, and man is required to be a willing co-worker. If we trusted to our own strength we should find it weakness, and even our own motives would be deceptive. We always need help from on high, and we always receive it if our good works are seasoned with grace. The broad and universal direction of the apostle is: "Work out your own salvation with fear and trembling; for it is God which worketh in you both to will and to do of his good pleasure." Thus we see that works which are approved of God are so much under his direction that they necessarily partake of a degree of holiness; and while we do not perform them as meritorious, our Heavenly Father may reward them as he chooses without breaking any law of his kingdom.

Our Heavenly Father is much more explicit as to how he will treat our works after death than before death. Perhaps it is because we would all our days be subject to vanity in this life, if we knew how our Lord was rewarding our faithfulness; but when we die and go hence we will have a better mind and a truer appreciation of all that is said and done in our behalf. Perhaps the greatest surprise to the righteous in the heavenly world will be the reason given for these words addressed to them: "Come, ye blessed of my Father, inherit the kingdom prepared for you from the foundation of the world." The reason is that they had been feeding Christ when he was hungry, and giving him drink when he was thirsty, and furnishing him room and lodging when he was a stranger, and clothing him when he was destitute, and visiting him when he was sick and in prison; and all this was done for the Lord by doing the same things to the least Christians. Here every good deed of life seems to be freighted with blessings on the doer as soon as he enters the paradise of God. Just as the Book of God closes we read the assuring words: "Blessed are they that do his commandments, that they may have right to the tree of life, and may enter in through the gates into the city." John, in the Gospel, testifies that his commandment is life everlasting. In the Revelation he testifies that the tree of life is near the river of life, and bears twelve manner of fruits, yielding her fruit every month; and the leaves of the tree are for the healing of the nations. Can we imagine the blessedness of receiving such heavenly possessions for an obedience which is easy and safe to the soul in all its terms and requirements? We ought to obey God rather than men. "Let us hear the conclusion of the whole matter: Fear God, and keep his commandments; for this is the whole duty of man."

The nature of good works is twofold—first, they have their origin and strength in the appointment and grace of God; secondly, they live only in hearts and lives willing to do the will of God.

First. Our good works are from God. Paul says that the God of peace works in us "that which is well-pleasing in his sight through Christ Jesus." Then even in our obedience God honors his Son, and gives us the chief direction in all that we do. Isaiah proclaims this truth in these words: "Lord, thou wilt ordain peace for us; for thou also hast wrought all our works in us." The Saviour said: "My peace I leave with you." And it is worthy of note that in the two scriptures just quoted peace is shown to be the fruit of good works. War and divisions and error follow every evil way, while peace and unity of the Spirit and truth follow good works when they are wrought in us by Christ.

Men never claim any merit in works as procuring salvation until they take them away from God and undertake their performance by their own wisdom and strength. This is done when the direct witness of the Holy Spirit on the heart is ignored, and a study of the Scriptures, as to sacraments, ordinances, modes, times, and design, is set up as the fulfilling of the law concerning good works. Our sufficiency is of God. He is our strength in weakness and our light in darkness. Every prayer that we offer signifies that our works need help from on high. Unless God be in our works, and his Holy Spirit gives us the blessings desired in our petitions, prayer is a most unmeaning ceremony.

Secondly. All works receiving a reward from heaven must come from a willing mind. "Whatsoever thy hand findeth to do, do it with thy might," and do it willingly. The Lord loveth a cheerful giver. Remember that we are co-workers with God, and on his part he does all for us willingly. He asks us to have the same mind that was in Christ. He said of himself: "My meat is to do the will of him that sent me, and to finish his work." In the same cheerful spirit we should begin, continue, and finish the whole work of our Christian pilgrimage. Then we may sing:

"I have fought my way through,
I have finished the work thou didst give me to do."

The necessity for good works is also twofold—first, to do the will of God; secondly, to bless others with our benefactions.

First. It is the will of God that our lives should be employed in doing good works. To the minister he says, "Feed my sheep; feed my lambs"—Feed the flock over which the Holy Ghost hath made you overseer; but do not be such an overseer as to lord it over God's heritage. If any man would be minister let him be the servant of all. To the

Church he says, "Be kindly affectioned one to another with brotherly love"—Be given to hospitality, distributing to the necessity of saints; live peaceably with all men; feed your enemy when he is hungry, and give him drink when he is thirsty.

The will of God is the beginning and end of all moral obligation. If reference were had to that will when we are tempted to indulge in bad works—such as the theater, the dance, the show, the card-table, the saloon—we would have a ready solution to every question of right and wrong. We would find that the will of God was our holiness. To reach this state we would find that it was necessary to abstain from all appearance of evil. The psalmist said: "I delight to do thy will, O my God; yea, thy law is within my heart." Whether the words be applied to Christ or himself, they are equally forcible and pertinent. From the will of God proceeds the law of God; and the law is holy, just, and good. Let the will of God be the criterion of every action, and Christian perfection will be gained and good works will stand as a city set on a hill, seen of all beholders.

Secondly. To bless others with our benefactions makes good works a necessity in the Christian life. No man liveth unto himself. Why should he, when so many are in want? why should he, when the heathen world to this day lieth in wickedness? why should he, when the poor we have always with us?

What else than Christian liberality will distribute equally and prudently food, clothing, and shelter? Sin-cursed as it is, this world may be the garden of the Lord by universal benevolence. Christ cared for us—let us care for others.

> Thou all our works in us hast wrought,
>   Our good is all divine;
> The praise of every virtuous thought
>   And righteous word is thine.

OUR LORD'S PARABLES.

The Pharisee and Publican.

"And he spake this parable unto certain which trusted in themselves that they were righteous, and despised others: Two men went up into the temple to pray; the one a Pharisee, and the other a publican. The Pharisee stood and prayed thus with himself, God, I thank thee that I am not as other men are, extortioners, unjust, adulterers, or even as this publican. I fast twice in the week, I give tithes of all that I possess. And the publican, standing afar off, would not lift up so much as his eyes unto heaven, but smote upon his breast, saying, God be merciful to me a sinner. I tell you this man went down to his house justified rather than the other: for every one that exalteth himself shall be abased; and he that humbleth himself shall be exalted." Luke xviii. 9–14.

TWO persons, a Pharisee and a publican, appear in this parable as the representatives of two religious views which are more controverted than any known among men. Those who rely upon a literal performance of duties and good works for salvation, and those who rely entirely upon the grace of God as manifested in the mediation of Jesus Christ, are represented. The first religious controversy in the world was between two brothers, Cain and Abel, ending in murder, and involving the issue here stated. Abel brought an offering full of shed blood, which looked to the coming of Christ, whose blood would cleanse from all sin; while Cain brought the fruit of the ground, and perhaps the very best fruit, as an offering unto the Lord. Unto both Cain and his offering God had no respect. Without the shedding of blood there could be no remission of sins. Unto Abel and his offering God had respect. In both instances the man and the offering are named together, the character of the latter determining the fate of the former. Cain's obedience was prompt and liberal enough, but it omitted reconciliation by shed blood and divine grace. He trusted in himself that he was righteous. Certain persons in the presence of Jesus had the same opinion of their own goodness and merits, and this false theory of justification led the Saviour in his own way by parable to set forth the difference between these two systems of religious faith. We think the introductory statement preceding the parable shows clearly that we have taken the right view of its meaning. And he spake this parable unto certain which *trusted in themselves that they were righteous* and depised others.

The Pharisee in the parable represents all who rely upon good works and obedience to specific commands for salvation. He is presented as the very best of the class. Error begets extremes, and it is easy to run back on the line from those who almost recognize the necessity of the witness of the Spirit and the atonement of Christ to those who believe the Universalist theory of the salvation of all men, or to those who rely upon morality and honesty. Even truth may be carried to extreme conclusions and become error. From the true doctrine of a general atonement made by our Lord for all men and spiritual regeneration, men have proceeded to the theory of unconditional election and reprobation, and to all the absurdities of Antinomianism.

Our Lord brings forth in detail all the good qualities of the Pharisee that we may see how many real virtues a man may possess in company with such sad defects as will leave him in the gall of bitterness and the bond of iniquity. Let us make a special inspection of his character on the praiseworthy side.

1. In the midst of the errors of the schools and the sects it was a virtue to be a Pharisee. The age was cultivated and inquisitive, and the human mind had a tendency to run into all extremes, foster every variety of speculation, and from these to fill the land with error. To preserve the most orthodox faith in the midst of a heterodox period was a thing not to be despised. The Pharisee believed in God, in the inspiration of the Scriptures of the Old Testament, and in the resurrection of the dead to be

rewarded or punished according to the deeds done in the body. He kept the temple of the Lord, and ostensibly he was the true worshiper. Fastings, giving of alms, prayers, and attending the sanctuary were strictly observed.

2. Some things commendatory may be observed of the Pharisee as to his occupation at the time. He was found in the house of God, and apparently for the purpose of prayer. Here was the right place to pray, as the Lord had declared that his house should be called the house of prayer. The Pharisees had two days in the week set apart for prayer —Monday and Thursday—and not one day as the Christian Churches have, and this man was attending on one of those days. He was in the temple, without the attraction of a minister to address an audience with words of eloquence, or a company of singers to discourse sweet music, or a congregation of well-dressed people for observation and conversation; but he went alone, entered the house, took his place, and in his way performed his routine of duties. Here are points of good conduct that will make some professors of religion blush, and will keep this Pharisee from indiscriminate and wholesale censure and criticism. Let us give him due credit for all that he did worthy of praise, censuring him only for his defects, and escaping their imitation.

3. Let us notice specific acts of character belong-

ing to this Pharisee. He fasted twice in the week. Fasting was a religious duty so well established in the days of our Lord that he left it to be observed without a specific command, and even answered the complaint made against his disciples because they did not fast. We have the command of the apostles in its favor, which forbids any questioning as to the duty or the benefits derived from it to our spiritual growth. We have known a few persons whose physical condition was such that they could not fast without producing sickness; but there are not many who cannot fast. Here was a man who was only a formal worshiper who fasted twice in the week, while many churches do not require or practice fasting more than four times a year, appointing the day before a quarterly or sacramental meeting when the holy communion will be administered. We do not doubt that the sacrament of the Lord's Supper was observed by the early Christians once a week, while now it is only kept monthly or quarterly by many churches.

4. He gave tithes of all that he possessed. One of the hardest lessons to teach even Christian men is that their goods and themselves belong to the Lord. When God allowed his tenants nine-tenths of the produce of the field, shop, and office, and demanded only one-tenth for the use of his Church, he showed a liberality that was surprising to all landlords. Not an instance like it can be found in

the annals of any nation. But what do we see as the result of this generosity. Giving men so nearly all that is made, and leaving them free to withhold the small part named if they will at their peril, finds the great majority inclined to withhold and keep all. We doubt whether there is a Christian Church in the world to-day that could support itself financially on the voluntary, free-will principle of action. Officers, collectors, and pleaders are found to be essentially necessary to draw from reluctant purses the meager contributions which the Church realizes for the gospel at home and abroad. It is probable that the single and sinful article of tobacco alone costs the Church, as a voluntary and wicked extravagance, more than all amounts received for the cause of God after all the importunate entreaties of ministers and official laymen. But this Pharisee, of his own free will and accord, gave tithes of all that he possessed.

5. This Pharisee was not an extortioner. While this was true as to the Pharisee, he asserts it by making a mean reflection on the publican. The office of the publican was to collect the Roman revenues, and in it there was ample opportunity to be guilty of extortion in demanding more taxes than were due, and in seizing more property than would pay the taxes. This made the publicans specially odious to the Jews. The Jews stood to the Roman Government very much as the American colonies

stood to the English Government at the time of our declaration of independence, being subject to taxation without representation. Having no representation in Parliament, it is easy to see how our taxes would be increased beyond a due proportion, and the collecting officers, having but little sympathy with our country and people, would be apt to be guilty of extortion. There were many publicans in Judea at the time, and the very name was despised by the Jews. Zaccheus was the chief of the publicans, and seemed to suppose that the first suspicion concerning him would be that he was an extortioner, and hence he offered to restore to the injured fourfold if they could prove him guilty. Matthew also was a publican of an inferior grade.

The wisdom of any government is seen in equality of taxation. This is one of the greatest difficulties in legislation, and one of the strongest reasons for giving every district its own chosen representation. Our country, as a rule, has admirably observed this equality—taxing property, offices, and the like the same in amount; but no little difficulty is experienced in doing exact justice to all sections and interests where they are unlike each other in industrial pursuits. The late war caused an enormous increase of taxation, and since peace came it has required many years to readjust this subject to its normal condition.

But whatever the motive of the Pharisee was toward the publican, it was a good quality to be free from extortion. Being probably a rich man and a man of influence, he had opportunities to commit this sin. O how many men do not hesitate openly and boldly to make all the money possible out of their own abundance and others' necessities! How few Christians would refuse to join a monopoly to buy or sell leading articles of trade so as to increase or decrease the price! Many engage in the late style of margins, whereby they become gamblers outright. We give this Pharisee credit for being no extortioner, and present him as a worthy example superior to many professors of religion who suppose that they excel him in all virtues.

6. Our Pharisee was not unjust. It would be an interesting inquiry, if it had any possible solution, to ask how many debts would be paid voluntarily if all the coercive power of the law to enforce payment were removed. We doubt whether twenty-five per cent. of all the private and public indebtedness of any country would be paid on this plan. Or how many public functionaries would be true to their trust if it were not for their oaths of office, their fear of punishment for perjury, and the liabilities of friends as security on their bonds? We reach the seat of total depravity in a few short steps in the direction indicated. But here was a man whose word was his bond, and who could appeal to his neighbors in proof that he observed his con-

tracts without mortgages, collaterals, or indorsers. He must have been a model man in his community, and no doubt laid the flattering unction to his soul that his good works would save him. A long business life, attended with large experience and observation, convinces us that a man strictly just from principle and not from policy is the exception and not the rule. Before this Pharisee is denounced by any one, we advise him to retrospect his business life with care, and see if it has been marked with complete justice to all men. Our Church has an excellent direction to her members: "Not to use many words in buying and selling." How few persons make exactly the same representation of an article as buyer of it and as seller! Many men take a different view of collecting the debts due to themselves and paying the debts that they owe. To be just, candid, sincere, truthful to the letter, are cardinal Christian virtues.

7. He was not an adulterer. The secret history that came to light by our Saviour of the guilty men who brought the woman to him under the guise of great piety indicates that the sin of adultery was common in that age. This fact makes the virtuous life of this man stand forth brighter and more praiseworthy than it would if the entire community had been chaste and innocent. We doubt whether any sin is more common than this sin, and this remark applies to all countries—civilized and

barbarous, Christian and pagan, and to all times, ancient and modern. The laws of God and man have not effected its suppression. In our judgment only one thing can accomplish this most desirable end. The face of society must be set against this crime when committed by men with as much abhorrence and detestation as when women are the offenders.

What a number of virtues this Pharisee possessed, all to be overshadowed by one fatal mistake! Our first parents made but one mistake, and it produced their and our ruin. The foolish virgins made only one mistake in not providing oil enough to last until midnight, and they were left in darkness. Peter made but one mistake when he denied his Lord, but the result was that he went and wept bitterly. The rich man only allowed one beggar to starve at his gate, "and in hell he lifted up his eyes, being in torments." This Pharisee made but one mistake, in *trusting in himself* that he was a justified man; and with this self-complacency he could not enter his own door a justified man in the eyes of Christ the Judge. He trusted in himself that he was righteous. He was actually righteous as he supposed in his nature and in his life, and of course he was neither depraved in part nor entirely. All his works were meritorious and pleasing to contemplate, and his family connections, Church relationship, and natural and cultivated goodness made him as he thought one of Heaven's chief favorites. But how does the word of God depict the moral nature and life of this Pharisee and of every other unregenerate man? The imaginations of the thoughts of their hearts are evil, and only evil, and that continually; "the carnal mind is enmity against God;" "the whole head is sick, and the whole heart faint;" "the heart is deceitful above all things, and desperately wicked;" "their throat is an open sepulcher;" "with their tongues they have used deceit;" "the poison of asps is under their lips;" their mouth is full of cursing and bitterness;" "their feet are swift to shed blood." Such is the faithful and fearful picture drawn from the Bible of every man before he turns to God and lives through his Son.

Righteousness is the highest moral and spiritual excellence found in any heart. It is heaven-born, for the Lord "is made unto us righteousness." It is not of earth, for "there is none righteous; no, not one." "Our own righteousness is as filthy rags." "True righteousness is of faith, for the righteousness of God is by faith of Jesus Christ unto all, and upon all them that believe."

What a radical and fundamental mistake this Pharisee made in this one particular! His undue estimate of his own virtues sealed his heart against holiness and developed a character guilty and even pitiable in the extreme. Notice first that he despised others. He not only had a low opinion of those who were below him in social position, or who belonged to another sect or party, but he despised them with scorn and contempt. His hatred showed itself in the house of God, and in his very prayers. From thoughts to words his hatred vented itself, and took unseemly form. The whole race of publicans he despised, and he had but to see one to express his opinion to God and men evincing extreme aversion. Some one has said that we never find our friends as good nor our enemies as bad as we had supposed. Certainly judging a man by his name, or his Church, or his theory, or his party, is a very unsafe test of character. The very best and greatest men sometimes spring from the most unpromising families, while those raised in affluence and having every social advantage, with the best religious culture, may become the most degraded and worthless. Individual character tested by its own works is the only safe criterion.

The defect named not only showed in this Pharisee a hatred of other men, but it also exhibited in his prayers such qualities as marked the man utterly destitute of pure and undefiled religion. The whole manner and bearing of his address is in proof. He addresses God with no reverence or solemnity, but very much as if the Lord were the presiding officer of some society appointed to applaud his merits. "God, I thank thee," has no more meaning than if he had said, "Mr. President." The claim of equality of rights with God is almost asserted. He claimed the right of private judgment in his own case as to his moral and religious qualities. And there is not an intimation of any possible defect in his own life, or of possible good in the life of the publican.

Again, the necessary qualities of repentance and faith are sadly wanting—the first being entirely unknown, and the last being only historical and general. He shows no repentance toward God. Being free from sin in his own opinion, he has no cause for repentance. So much as one misspent day or hour of his life, or one mistake or evil deed, is unacknowledged. His life is one of unclouded prosperity and unblurred morality. Such purity made it unnecessary, in his judgment, to have personal and abiding faith in Christ. The necessity for a vicarious atonement for his sins he has never perceived. His God, in whom he believes, is really more the God of the deist than the God of the Christian.

Here we have the best example of literal and exact obedience to duties as the procuring cause for the remission of sins that we may hope to find; and yet ignoring the grace of God and the blood of Jesus as the efficient and meritorious cause, we see how inadequate is their claim. It would be unjust to God and unsafe to our souls to make our obedience the means of our own salvation. Every act of our own we would flatter with the assurance that it was perfect in mode, intention, and performance, while prejudice and predilection may have determined us in favor of the wrong mode; self-will might be mistaken for purity of intention, and performance might be under the influence of times and seasons until a life of the greatest irregularity would follow.

We now reach a subject as important to sinful man as any that he is ever called to consider. How is the sinner justified? How may one who is "dead in trespasses and sins" live again? How may one living without hope and without God in the world be assured that he has found restoration to the divine favor?

> How can a sinner know
> His sins on earth forgiven?
> How can my gracious Saviour show
> My name inscribed in heaven?

The publican will give us the needed information. We will find that man is saved by grace through faith in Christ.

We might ask many questions about the publican, and from a better motive than idle curiosity. He may have had some religious teaching in early life that he threw off with manhood, and after running a decade or a score of years or more in sin these had returned to his conscience and memory with unusual power. The memory of a mother's prayers when a boy, or her dying injunctions as he reached manhood, may have possessed his soul, producing deep contrition. Some late bereavement of his own may have been the cause of disturbing his whole moral nature with the consciousness of his guilt. Possibly he had buried a daughter or a son whom he loved as the apple of his eye; or some visitation of God upon the land for its sins may have been before his eyes, warning him that it is a fearful thing to fall into the hands of the living God. He may have been reviewing his own sinful life, and while he was amazed and shocked at the number and heinousness of his crimes, the Spirit of God sealed deep and timely conviction in his soul. We do not know the immediate cause of his conviction at the temple, but we do know that he is introduced to us by the Master as being deeply penitent on account of his sins, which is the first step toward his recovery.

We gain insight enough into his condition to believe that he was neither in the lowest nor the highest class of society. He had an office and a house. A publican was a tax-collector for a certain district, and he would not be intrusted with the revenues of the government unless he was responsible and reliable. He had a home of his own, as he went down to his house justified. So we judge that he was in the middle station of life, having neither poverty nor riches, but caring for his family and attending to his business as an industrious and prudent man.

For the masses of any population this middle state is the best for temporal and spiritual welfare.

The publican was in great agony on account of the peril of his soul. He knew that the temple was the appointed place for prayer, and he went thither. But his sense of his unworthiness was so oppressive that he was standing afar off from the favorite and conspicuous places of the house, and sought to offer his prayer in the vestibule or court allotted to the Gentiles and the unworthy. His contrition of soul became so violent that he did not so much as lift up his eyes to heaven. He looked to the dust where he expected soon to go, rather than to heaven above where he scarcely dared to hope that he might ascend. He smote with his hand upon his guilty breast, as representing the depraved heart that he was fully conscious of possessing. Here we have all the possible manifestations and evidences of a penitent sinner—humble prayer, conscious guilt and shame, and yet daring to approach God in faith. Of him it might be said in that moment: "There is joy in heaven in the presence of the angels of God over one sinner that repenteth."

His prayer is more conspicuous for its fullness than for its brevity. In the fewest words he condenses his request, replete with all that he could desire. With awful reverence he called on God, speaking his name as if he dreaded to utter it. His infinite attributes he does not dare to consider one by one. If he should think a moment of his omnipotence, and behold God taking up the isles as a very little thing, he would sink beneath the sight. He dare not venture to contemplate the omnipresence of God, so as to behold him literally filling the universe with his own fullness. The omniscience of God would overawe his soul, if he should behold him as having all possible wisdom. He tries in his own weakness and guilt to approach feebly and touch the hem of his garment so that he might receive virtue. This he did, and no more; and thus he addressed God in prayer.

See how this troubled soul regarded himself. "Me, a sinner," is the brief and full confession of his guilt. He did not think of any nice calculation, whether he was born in sin, or became a sinner by association or example or preference, or whether part of his nature might be exempt from the taint. It seemed to him that he was overwhelmed in guilt. If he contemplated the extent of his guilt, he would exclaim, "I the chief of sinners am!" No doubt he would have acknowledged that from the crown of his head to the soles of his feet there were "wounds and bruises and putrefying sores." He knew that he had a desperate disease, and did not seek to hide it. It overwhelmed him to such a degree that he had not one word of retaliation for the proud Pharisee who stood taunting him at the very moment. He knew that "they that be whole need not a physician, but they that are sick;" and he believed that there was balm in Gilead and a physician there even for his troubled soul.

"Me" embraced all that he prayed for on that day. This was an hour when he might withdraw his requests from all others than himself. Usually in our prayers we are to remember others, but in that hour of extreme solicitude, when we seek to live and not die, and when we strive to escape from the guilt and pollution of sin to regeneration of soul and holiness of life, we may confine our petitions to a throne of mercy to our own pressing necessities. When Peter was sinking he could only plead, "Lord, save, or I perish!" When the man was blind his petition was, "Lord, that I may receive my sight!" When Saul was struck to the earth we hear the exclamation, "Lord, what wilt thou have me to do?" When Stephen was dying his last request was, "Lord Jesus, receive my spirit." The special object sought by the publican was mercy. It has been said that a time will be reached in every man's life when mercy will seem to him the darling attribute of the Deity. No man may hope for mercy without being merciful. "Blessed are the merciful, for they shall obtain mercy." And this quality in God is so abundant that the psalmist in one Psalm affirms twenty-six times that "his mercy endureth forever." In proportion to the guilt of the sinner, and his knowledge and acknowledgment of it, will

The Pharisee and Publican. 189

be his realizing sense of the value of the mercy of God. A knowledge of the heinousness of sin will beget a knowledge of the amazing goodness of God in showing mercy toward the sinner. As human laws recognize the propriety of punishing men with death or with years of imprisonment for a single offense, how much graver must a life of sin appear to God when we remember that he cannot look upon sin with the least allowance?

"The publican went down to his house justified." He was justified in the very hour that he prayed. Did not the recorder of names in the Lamb's book of life write his name therein and append to it, "justified?" He was acquitted, discharged, released from sin, and became a new creature in Christ Jesus. He realized that being justified by faith he had peace with God through his Lord Jesus Christ. He was justified by the grace of the Lord. No man is justified by the law; so that he did not have a merely formal or legal acquittal, but a gracious deliverance through faith, being justified, from all things from which he could not be justified by the law of Moses. As the law of Moses was a law divinely inspired, if any enactments of law could have justifying virtue those laws would possess it; but by the deeds of the law, even of the best and holiest law, shall no flesh be justified. By believing in Jesus the sinner is justified. What a happy hour to the publican when for the first time in his life he went to his house and told the family that he was justified! He could then say, "The Spirit itself beareth witness with my spirit that I am a child of God."

We have finished the comparison and the contrast between the two systems—salvation by grace and salvation by works. The former leads to present safety and future blessedness in heaven, the latter to deceptive self-righteousness and future abandonment to the punishment of the wicked. True repentance and implicit faith in God characterize the former, bigotry and pride mark the conduct of the latter. Choose ye to-day between truth and error. Choose the truth and live.

The Unjust Judge.

"And he spake a parable unto them to this end, that men ought always to pray, and not to faint; saying, There was in a city a judge which feared not God, neither regarded man; and there was a widow in that city, and she came unto him, saying, Avenge me of mine adversary. And he would not for awhile; but afterward he said within himself, Though I fear not God, nor regard man; yet because this widow troubleth me, I will avenge her, lest by her continual coming she weary me. And the Lord said, Hear what the unjust judge saith. And shall not God avenge his own elect, which cry day and night unto him, though he bear long with them? I tell you that he will avenge them speedily. Nevertheless, when the Son of man cometh, shall he find faith on the earth?" Luke xviii. 1-8.

IN this parable the key hangs at the door. We find inscribed on it, "Men ought always to pray, and not to faint." This gives us the subject in advance, and as we unlock and open room after room the theme of prayer is constantly in our minds. Usually in our Lord's parables we are invited into the building, and after examining all its parts we sum up its beauties and its designs; but here we are greatly assisted in having a single subject for our meditations, and that one of unsurpassed practical importance.

Our subject is prayer. Faith falters here sooner

than at any other point. To use the words of prayer and have no assured confidence that there is a direct connection between the acts of God and the petition offered is common, while to have such confidence requires a high degree of grace and trust. Ten thousand prayers are unanswered through want of faith. Whoever has faith in prayer can easily have faith in all the doctrines of the Bible. We open our remarks on this parable by giving in this place an article which we wrote and published some years ago in the *Central Methodist*, and which Bishop McTyeire was kind enough to indorse in a private note sent us:

PRAYER A STUDY.

As prayer is our daily duty and privilege, it is best to study it in several points of view. Its manner and spirit are essential to be known as well as any mistakes to which we may be liable when we pray. One of the disciples of Jesus said to him one day: "Lord, teach us to pray, as John also taught his disciples." (Luke xi. 1.) The request was made just as our Lord ceased praying in a certain place, and no doubt it was his example at the time which suggested the matter to the mind of the disciple. We may infer that John specially instructed his disciples in the manner and matter of prayer, as of prime importance. It will be seen that the request of the disciple named above caused the Lord to repeat a part of his Sermon on the Mount, beginning with the manner of prayer.

The manner of prayer is admirably shown in the Sermon on the Mount. Our Lord says, "After this manner therefore pray ye." Not essentially the same words at all times, but study like brevity, comprehensiveness, and want of repetition. Then follows the model: "Our Father which art in heaven, hallowed be thy name." Let every prayer begin with recognizing God, and close with asking the object desired through Jesus Christ. As there is no other name given under heaven by which we may be saved, we should ever hallow the name of God. "Thy kingdom come." This is the first request, and it should be our first desire that the kingdom of Christ should reach to the ends of the earth. The missionary spirit is to be felt and acknowledged in the first petition. "Thy will be done on earth as it is in heaven." God must rule the nations, and he must reign supreme in each heart. Personal purity will lead to national renovation. "Give us this day our daily bread." The spread of the gospel and personal holiness precede the first meal of the day. There is no virtue in poverty, as we may pray for our daily bread, standing here for the necessaries of life. "And forgive us our debts as we forgive our debtors." Debts, trespasses, and sins are used synonymously, as will be seen by comparing Matthew vi. 12, xiv. 15, and

xviii. 21, 22. "And lead us not into temptation, but deliver us from evil." Lead us, O Lord, this day, but not into temptation, and in mercy deliver us from all evil. These two are the only exemptions named in the prayer. Remember that the gospel sent abroad and holiness of heart and life are asked before we petition for bread, or forgiveness, or deliverance from temptation or evil. What an excellent model of prayer in a few sentences—so comprehensive, so plain, so brief, so personal and practical!

The spirit of our prayer is explained by our Lord in a single sentence: "But thou, when thou prayest, enter into thy closet, and when thou hast shut thy door, pray to thy Father which is in secret." (Matthew vi. 6.) Enter the closet and shut the door before you pray. If you are praying in the great congregation do this first, and then address God and not the people. One might enter the closet and leave an open door to be seen of men. The true spirit suggests that all external hinderances be removed, and then the heart is prepared to address God alone, asking for the blessings that it needs.

We note some mistakes to which we are liable when we pray:

1. We are not to seek a conspicuous place. Christ said of some: "They love to pray standing in the synagogues and in the corners of the streets."

The street-corners were for the more ambitious—the synagogues for those who could content themselves with a few hearers. Both are exactly opposite in spirit to the closet as a place of prayer. When Jesus was at Gethsemane he said to the disciples: "Sit ye here while I go and pray yonder. And he went a little farther, and fell on his face and prayed; and he went away again the second time and prayed; and he left them and went away again and prayed the third time, saying the same words." (Matthew xxvi. 36–44.) Each time he left the crowd and went out alone to pray. This was his usual custom, sometimes expressed by going apart, sometimes by going into a mountain, and sometimes continuing alone in prayer all night.

2. We are not to use vain repetitions when we pray. (Matthew vi. 7.) Repetition is not the thing prohibited, as our daily wants will ever be the same, and may be expressed in the same words. Our Lord prayed the same words in the example given above. It is *vain* repetitions, such as the heathen used, which we are to avoid. The heathen were accustomed to repeat many times, "Great is Diana of the Ephesians," or "O Baal, hear us," or similar expressions, to excite their minds to attention. The papists use vain repetitions in their *Ave Marias* and *Paternosters*. Sometimes the preacher may do the same thing in spending some minutes in descriptions of the Deity.

3. We are to avoid periodical praying. "Pray without ceasing" is Paul's direction. We should ever be in a frame of supplication to God, for we are ever needy. When has one ceased to pray? We answer, When a single day and night have passed over his head without petitioning the Lord for mercies needed. A good man will pray morning, noon, and night, or oftener. We have no right to state our desires by the month, or the year, as if the Lord would furnish a wholesale supply. Do not many professors rely on the public Sunday prayers as a supply for the week? It is related of Dr. Franklin, when a boy, that he asked his father when laying in provisions for the season to say grace over them all at once to save time. Do not many Christians pursue this course, or omit possibly even the wholesale blessing?

4. "Not as I will, but as thou wilt," should be the spirit of every prayer. If Jesus could properly use these words, much more can weak and fallible men. The advantage is twofold. We have the wisdom of God and not our own, and the request may be granted, but not in our way or at our time. We see but a part; the Lord comprehends all—past, present, future. From our petition he understands our desires, and from his infinite wisdom and resources he directs the answer. It is said that Augustine's mother prayed daily for his conversion. He was wild, and she was uneasy. He

desired to visit Italy, and she opposed it. He went, and was converted in Milan. Augustine said afterward about his mother's prayers: "Thou didst deny her what she prayed for then, that thou mightest grant her what she prayed for always."

We close. Let the Bible-reader search and find other scripture directions concerning the character of true prayer and the errors to which we are liable.

The parables of our Lord usually proceed by comparison, but this is one of contrast. The object is to show an instance of success where there was the greatest improbability that success would follow effort, and from thence to demonstrate the certainty of an answer to prayers offered to our merciful Heavenly Father. No characters stand more at antipodes than God our Judge and the unjust judge of this parable. In the character of the unjust judge there is not a single redeeming trait. We saw many good qualities in the Pharisee, but here we can find none. As the barren fig-tree did not produce one fig in three years, so here a man high in judicial authority has not one commendable feature of his whole life. We notice his character.

The judge had judicial authority in a whole city; either by appointment or election he had exclusive rights of his office, and those of a character which involved the rights of others in life, reputation, and property. To secure those rights to others he had taken the oaths belonging to his office and given all the pledges of which the subject was capable; and yet the name "unjust judge" will rest upon him forever. Look at the particulars.

He feared not God.

He had neither reverential nor servile fear of God. He had taken the oaths of his office in the name of God without any regard for his Creator. Doubtless he believed if God existed he had but little to do with the affairs of this world, and that all men irrespective of character were equally safe after death. This led him to adopt a course where policy and not principle governed all his actions. Such a life would answer for a period of health and a time of safety, but for sickness and danger it had no provision of comfort. We once knew a fine scholar who was a professed infidel. One day he had declared in our presence that he would prefer hell to heaven in the future in the event that he could rank with Bolingbroke, Voltaire, and Hume in intellect in the abode of lost spirits, stating that he could not endure heaven with the pious songs such as the churches employed. We assured him that he stood a fair chance to select his residence, but we doubted whether he could ever reach the desired equality of rank with the leading infidels named. Soon after that time the horses ran away with the stage-coach which was full of passengers, and our infidel one of the party. The company said that he prayed audibly and earnestly from the moment that he knew of the danger they were in to the moment when the danger was passed. A man who fears not God is lost to all sense of proper fear. He may fear when the lightning peels the oak at his side because of his proximity to bodily danger, but he would not fear to take a bribe in secret if he were a judge.

Holy writ assures us that the fear of the Lord is the beginning of wisdom. Without it all life is folly. The fear of the Lord is clean, enduring forever. It has in it no dregs of moral impurity, and it continues in eternity. One who fears the Lord aright perceives his justice to be as proper as his mercy. But this judge feared not God.

Another quality belonging to this judge was that he regarded not man. He was a sinner who knew his own character. Many men either do not know themselves or will not acknowledge their evil ways; but this man, perhaps with no shame in his soul, said of himself that he neither feared God nor regarded man. How shameful the character which he possessed!

Only the worst men ever become so hardened as to be indifferent to public opinion. The judgment of a community about each citizen, when all the facts are known, is generally right. The good man meets with approval, the bad man is under suspicion and censure. The lash of public odium is applied to the latter every day. If some horrible deed is done in darkness, he is suspected. He is far gone in obduracy when he ceases to regard public opinion concerning himself. The innocent cannot bear the suspicion of their guilt. Sometimes they die under a charge wrongfully made. This judge had no regard for the truthful accusations which were laid at his door. How infamous his character!

He is known to this day by the title "the unjust judge." How great the difference between a just and an unjust judge! An ancient king passed a law against adultery, declaring that the offender should lose his sight. The first offender was his own son. Here the love of the father and the vindication of the law were in conflict. The unjust judge in the parable would have passed the offense, and thereby weakened all proper respect for the laws. But the king who passed this law was a just king. He brought his son before him, and had one of his own eyes taken out and one of the eyes of his son. So the law was kept inviolate, and the son must have seen his sin in a light never before considered.

We now see the character of the unjust judge. He was habitually unjust, and he neither feared God nor regarded man. How unlikely that any cause which depended solely on its own intrinsic merits would find favor in his eyes! He used filthy scales in weighing the law. Now if such a cause as we have named should be heard favorably by him without a bribe or undue influence, how much more certain is it that our God will hear his children when they cry unto him!

Our plea is not to a man who fears not God, but to the living and true God. He weighs and administers equity with a nicer adjustment than the finest scales of the apothecary. He is not only just, but he is full of compassion. He regards man so truly that "he gave his only-begotten Son that whosoever believeth on him might not perish, but have everlasting life." Any kind father would feel that if he had given a beloved son in sacrifice for another it was more than if he had given all his goods. Here God not only gave his Son for us in his own divine nature, but he clothed him with a human nature like our own, and gave him that nature for our race and for no other beings. "Will he not then with him freely give us all things?" He will certainly hear and answer our prayers.

In the particular instance that came before the unjust judge there were two sources of improbability not yet named. The pleader was a widow. Defenseless, unprotected, and without a vote at the polls or influence in the city, she was the importunate solicitor in the court. Her circumstances in life deprived her of money, and the law deprived her of power and influence. She had no attorney to plead for her, and knew not even the forms of the court. But she pleaded day after day. Her adversary was a man of the city, unjust as the judge was unjust, persecuting a poor widow—probably a man of wealth and social position, and having power and influence in every place. He seems to have paid no attention to the widow's pleading, so secure did he feel in the known injustice of the judge and his own powers. What added disadvantages and improbabilities of success are here named! Still she pleaded her cause, and succeeded by pleading her cause.

The elements of improbability here named before the unjust judge are those which will insure success before the Judge of all the earth. He is specially the God of the fatherless and the widow. He has appointed his Son to be the Advocate with the Father for all the helpless and dependent ones. He pleads in his Father's court, where he never asks without receiving, and where all the forms of the law are observed. He paid the debts of the helpless with his own blood. He avenges their cause against all such adversaries as oppress the widow and the orphan. He will not look upon their sins with any allowance. God will hear the plea of the innocent and answer from heaven.

In the decision of the unjust judge the sentence was right and the motive wrong. Many an act right in itself loses its reward by a wrong purpose in procuring it. A man may pay money into the treasury of the Lord to be rid of the collector and to be seen of men. Another may preach more to support himself and family than to save souls. We knew a man who proposed to unite with the Church in the town where he lived that would give him the most patronage in trade. Here, the case of the judge was his motive, and without any reference to the justice or injustice of the cause of the widow. He said, "I will decide for her, lest by her continual coming she weary me." It seemed to him that she would never cease to come. He had a good salary, was rich, and increased in goods, and possibly had a life estate in his office, and was saying to himself, "Soul, take thine ease," and he was unwilling to be disturbed. Possibly some feeble remains of conscience were in his breast, and the widow reached them, making him unhappy; and so he granted her request. The act was right, and the motive wrong. Let every one examine closely his motives in each step of life, for God judges more by intention than by overt acts.

Surely our Lord has convinced all, in this sharply drawn contrast between the justice and goodness of God and the injustice and servility of an unworthy earthly judge, that "men ought always to pray, and not to faint."

Men ought always to pray, because it is their duty to pray always. "Pray without ceasing" is the direction. The will and command of God are sufficient reasons for obedience at all times. We need ask no more than this: Hath God commanded? But here our pressing wants continue as long as the command to pray continues. In the morning we are in want, at noon we hunger, in the evening we thirst, at night we are enveloped with darkness, storms, and unseen dangers. The reason is apparent why we should always pray.

The privilege and the command to pray are to men, to all men. Whoever has wants may pray. Whoever is full, lacking nothing, may trust to that fullness. The wicked need not pray if he continues to trust in and practice his wickedness. In this event he would lack repentance and faith. No prayers are heard and answered when these are wanting. But the penitent sinner may pray, "God be merciful to me a sinner!"

Men may always pray, and not faint. The Lord's ear is not heavy that he cannot hear, nor his arm shortened that he cannot save. Why then should men faint when succor is at hand? A balm in Gilead and a physician there are ever present. Ten thousand testimonials exist that sin has been cured by the Great Physician. Look and live! Go boldly to the throne of grace, and obtain mercy and find grace to help in time of need.

The Wise and Foolish Virgins.

"Then shall the kingdom of heaven be likened unto ten virgins, which took their lamps, and went forth to meet the bridegroom. And five of them were wise, and five were foolish. They that were foolish took their lamps, and took no oil with them; but the wise took oil in their vessels with their lamps. While the bridegroom tarried, they all slumbered and slept. And at midnight there was a cry made, Behold, the bridegroom cometh; go ye out to meet him. Then all those virgins arose, and trimmed their lamps. And the foolish said unto the wise, Give us of your oil; for our lamps are gone out. But the wise answered, saying, Not so; lest there be not enough for us and you; but go ye rather to them that sell, and buy for yourselves. And while they went to buy, the bridegroom came; and they that were ready went in with him to the marriage; and the door was shut. Afterward came also the other virgins, saying, Lord, Lord, open to us. But he answered and said, Verily I say unto you, I know you not. Watch therefore; for ye know neither the day nor the hour wherein the Son of man cometh." Matt. xxv. 1-13.

IN the Gospel by John we have recorded, shortly before the betrayal and crucifixion of our Lord, his farewell sermon of *comfort* to his disciples. The consolatory words of that discourse are as precious as any known to earth. "Let not your heart be troubled; ye believe in God, believe also in me," is an average sample of the kind and encouraging words of Jesus. In the Gospel by Luke, shortly before the betrayal and crucifixion of our Lord, we have his farewell sermon of *caution* to his followers; and in the center of that discourse the parable of the wise and foolish virgins is recorded. Caution in a world of danger is as valuable and necessary as comfort in a world of hope and fear alternating. While the sermon recorded by John is more pleasant, the one recorded by Luke is equally important, and the more so because we are now in the Christian warfare.

This parable is laid in the most attractive of all human events—a marriage. In a great variety of forms and customs all ages and countries reach the same end in the numerous marriages which take place, and the unbounded joy occasioned by the event. But sadly we see at earth's most choice festivity one-half of the gay and happy ones lost in midnight darkness, and just at the moment when they had the most sanguine hopes of entering into the mansions of light. We are humbled under this view, and conclude that the world can afford no unmixed joy, no roses without thorns.

A Jewish marriage was one of taste and ceremony. It was customary to have ten witnesses at a marriage, or at the opening and dedication of a synagogue. The bridegroom chose and invited these witnesses in due time. They were to prepare

The Wise and Foolish Virgins. 207

together, dress alike, act in harmony, and have the same customs and observances. On the day of the celebration of the nuptials they were to meet at the house of the bridegroom, have all their preparation complete, and go together to meet the bridegroom, the bride, and their attendants, who were coming from the house of the bride. The marriage took place at the house of the bridegroom. Usually the time was at the rising of the evening star. Lighted lamps, held in the hand by the attendants, were used. Vessels containing oil, from which the lamps carried by the witnesses were supplied, were a necessary accompaniment. A herald was sent forth by the bridegroom and his party to announce their approach to the witnesses, that there might be no delay in the marriage ceremony and the festivities. This was literally the formula.

The lesson taught is the state of the Church militant, from its first call to duty and obedience to God to its entrance through the doors which open to admit the believer to eternal bliss and close on the hypocrite and self-deceived forever. Here we have a true picture of the Church in the aggregate, and of each individual member, whether saved or lost. . A truthful mirror shows not only the beauty of the face, but also its deformities. One who will not see the latter, but stands in pleasing admiration of the former, is injuring his own character when the painful truth is revealed, "Know thyself to-day, and to-morrow thou wilt not be a stranger to thyself."

In the admirably drawn picture of the wise and foolish virgins, what would first strike an observant Jew with greatest force? It would be the *likeness* that obtains between the two.

As soon as our Lord began speaking he named the number of each as being exactly equal. Ten was the number required at a Jewish marriage, and here five of them are found to be foolish. It was remarkable that the number was the same, as the character possessed was so different. Wisdom and folly stand at farthest antipodes. Their opportunities for improvement and their temptations to abuse their opportunities were also the same. Still one half were wise and the other half foolish; one half were saved and the other half lost. Just as we shall find in some families where the religious and educational training of the children are the same, some of them improve all their advantages, while others throw them away.

Again they were alike in their general character, being ten virgins. In the judgment of society they were of equal credit and virtue. So great was their credit that the bridegroom did not hesitate to select and invite the foolish as readily as the wise. God is always discerning and judging the heart, but man can only perceive the exterior of human character. Every Church will have in it foolish virgins, but the true Israel whom the Lord recognizes are all wise.

All these virgins had the same invitation from the same bridegroom. We have not yet reached any difference between them. The voice that said to the wise, "Come, for all things are now ready," spoke the same words to the foolish. It was not an urgent, pressing plea to those who were saved, and a half-reluctant invitation to the lost that caused the latter to hesitate, and then procrastinate making preparation, and then to fail because they were not ready. It was not a specific direction as to time and place and costume given to the wise that enabled them to prepare, while the foolish, lacking these things, were bewildered and lost. They were more like the members of the same church who had the same minister, the same doctrines, the same altar of prayer, the same hymns, the same sacraments, and even the same Bible, than they were like Calvinists and Arminians, or Catholics and Protestants.

In their understanding of all the particulars of the invitation and preparation they were alike. They agreed as to the dress and style in which each one should appear. Their preparations were made together, and by the mutual assistance of one another. They did not differ as to the length of time necessary for the preparation. They were ready to go forth to meet the bridegroom on the same day and at the same hour. None of these particulars can be assigned as any part of the reason for failure with the foolish virgins. There was no accusation of heresy on either side. With them there was no difference of opinion as to fundamental doctrines. No exclusive mode of baptism was alleged by the wise virgins, nor any close communion limited to themselves. No apostolical succession in the ministry was claimed. No Pharisaical righteousness was paraded for a moment.

The similarity between the two extended still farther than we have named. Each carried a lamp which indicated an open profession of religion. No one relied upon morality and honesty alone to take them to heaven. Nor did they postpone joining the Church until they were aged and near death. In the morning of life, while they were virgins, they enrolled their names visibly and publicly as belonging to the bridegroom. The lamps were not dry and destitute of oil, but for a time they were all trimmed and burning. The surprising cry of the foolish was, "Our lamps are gone out!" They had religion for a time, but they fell from grace.

They not only carried their lamps in their hands, but at their side they carried a vessel larger than the lamp that could hold a greater supply of oil. It was their design to be true Christians. But just here, for the first time, we catch a glimpse of the crowning folly of the foolish in allowing all external preparations to exceed the actual supply of oil in their vessels and grace in their hearts. They had the usual lamp and the larger vessel to hold oil, the right dress and the right day and the right company, but they had provided only enough oil to fill a single lamp, and that would burn out hours before midnight. How many Christians are like these, having abundant outside preparation for heaven, but very little of the Spirit and grace of God!

The resemblance continues. They walked together to meet the bridegroom along the same road. It was on the same afternoon of the same day. They were lovingly in each other's company. They agreed on the place where they should stop and await the coming of the bridegroom. They all slumbered together. As the night advanced they slept soundly at the same time. Together they heard the messenger when he said, "Behold, the bridegroom cometh." Each awoke at the same time. Each one arose and trimmed her lamp.

We doubt whether any resemblance between two objects or persons can be found where they were alike in as many respects as are here stated. A certain supply of oil was the only difference. The Spirit of God dwelling in their heart is the only difference between the real and nominal professors of religion. The wise virgins prepared their own hearts aright, but they could neither behold nor judge the hearts of the foolish. "The Lord alone trieth the reins and searcheth the hearts of the children of men." What a fatal difference existed between the two! It was unknown by all the ten until the last moment. Then the announcement was astounding, overwhelming. They might say, "Lord, Lord, have we not prophesied in thy name, and in thy name done many wonderful works," but the answer is returned, "I never knew you." The door is shut.

In all the Churches men and women are found who have only a name to live. They deceive their own hearts and the Church of God, and so live and die, possessing, as all believe, a good religious character. With complacency they may look back in a dying-hour upon a long line of performances, and trust more to them than to the blood of Christ. A funeral eulogium may be pronounced in which these performances are tabled with great parade and exactness. Earth may say a good man has fallen, but God knoweth. The rich man died in great credit, and was buried in purple and fine linen, and his brethren thought he had ascended to Abraham's bosom; but it was Lazarus who went thither, while the rich man "lifted up his eyes in hell, being in torments."

What a careful work is self-examination! It is far more important than the impossible task of examining our neighbor. It is more charitable and scriptural. Begin with your own heart, and see that it is right. Let all other preparation pass until this is complete. The husbandman examines the heart of the seed to determine the kind to cast into the ground. He knows that a rough exterior may cover a sound heart. "My son, give me thine heart," is the command of the Lord. A clock can no more run without weights or power than a man can be a Christian with an unclean heart. "A new heart will I give you," is the assurance of our God. Meet not the bridegroom without this adorning. Trimming a lamp avails nothing after the oil is extinguished. Midnight is too late an hour to buy oil.

A very common mistake was made by the foolish virgins when they discovered that their lamps had gone out. They supposed that the wise could divide with them, and thus supply oil for the ten. The grace of God that bringeth salvation is so personal that no one can safely give to another any quantity of the precious gift. And yet thousands believe that they will escape the damnation of hell in this way. A father's devotion to the Church and a mother's prayers, many children suppose, will secure them from danger, while they continue to roll sin under their tongues as a sweet morsel. No, indeed; each one must repent and believe for himself, and no exchange or appropriation of the piety of another is ever tolerated. We read of a man who was accustomed, when the minister or any person approached him on the subject of the salvation of his soul, to say, " My wife, Mary, prays for both of us." One night he dreamed that Mary and himself went hand in hand to the gate of heaven expecting to enter. Peter was at the gate, and as he opened it he said, "Come in, Mary, for both." The dreamer was left, and the gate was shut.

The evil of procrastination was seen in the history of the foolish virgins. They had many weeks and days given them for preparation, and one main duty to discharge in securing an abundant supply of oil, and this was the duty that was constantly postponed. At length when the last day arrived, and the sun had retired from sight, and the evening star had appeared, and even the hour of midnight approached, they were still unprepared. Midnight was the worst hour of the twenty-four to make preparation. All the shops where oil was sold were closed, and the shop-keepers were asleep. The door was opened only long enough to allow those who were ready to enter, and then on the unworthy it was shut forever. But "seek ye first the kingdom of God and his righteousness," is the command of Jesus. Satan answers: "Ye shall not surely die;

To-morrow shall as this day be, and more abundant."

Unusual privileges had been given to the foolish virgins. The bridegroom, the Lord Jesus, had invited them to his marriage. He gave them his

The Wise and Foolish Virgins. 215

elect saints—the wise virgins—as their companions. They had abundant time for preparation. They did all external work well. They were not prevented for a day by any calamity. Their associations were with the good to the last moment. But when discovery was made of their great want, unusual privileges were followed by unusual silence on the part of the Lord. The door was shut on them forever without a word. They were left speechless in outer darkness. In a single moment the wise entered and saw the glorious light of paradise, while the foolish fell in the blackness of night without sun, moon, or stars. "Why will ye die?"

The Rich Man and Lazarus.

"There was a certain rich man which was clothed in purple and fine linen, and fared sumptuously every day; and there was a certain beggar named Lazarus, which was laid at his gate, full of sores, and desiring to be fed with the crumbs which fell from the rich man's table; moreover, the dogs came and licked his sores. And it came to pass that the beggar died, and was carried by the angels into Abraham's bosom; the rich man also died and was buried, and in hell he lifted up his eyes, being in torments, and seeth Abraham afar off, and Lazarus in his bosom. And he cried and said, Father Abraham, have mercy on me, and send Lazarus, that he may dip the tip of his finger in water and cool my tongue, for I am tormented in this flame. But Abraham said, Son, remember that thou in thy life-time receivedst thy good things, and likewise Lazarus evil things; but now he is comforted and thou art tormented. And besides all this, between us and you there is a great gulf fixed: so that they which would pass from hence to you cannot; neither can they pass to us, that would come from thence. Then he said, I pray thee therefore, father, that thou wouldest send him to my father's house: for I have five brethren; that he may testify unto them, lest they also come into this place of torment. Abraham saith unto him, They have Moses and the prophets; let them hear them. And he said, Nay, father Abraham; but if one went unto them from the dead, they will repent. And he said unto him, If they hear not

The Rich Man and Lazarus.

Moses and the prophets, neither will they be persuaded, though one rose from the dead." Luke xvi. 19–31.

THIS parable differs from all the other parables of our Lord in giving the true character of good and bad men shortly after they die. Indeed, it is the only time when Christ raised the curtain at the grave and gave us the sight of eternity in the first hour that we enter its endless domains.

The parable is peculiar also in being a direct example and authority of our Lord for preaching a sermon concerning the dead. Here he gives us a plain and faithful discourse as to two men who had died near the same place and near the same time. No friend of either party had asked for the sermon. To the kindred of the rich man it would have been the direst insult, while poor Lazarus had no friends to give him a decent sepulture. But the Master without invitation sets the example of naming the dead personally in his discourse and of hiding neither virtues nor faults.

We have a class of men who seek to give this parable very mythical interpretations, and to stress the word *hell* with a light and temporary signification. In our mind, there is no doubt that our Lord had in his eye some particular family whom he would not name, as it is not important to keep a registry of lost souls. In this family there were six brethren, all living at their ease and in pleasure. The rich man named is a certain rich man, and not any rich man, and was perhaps the eldest and most influential of his family; and hence his sudden dread, when he found hell was a reality, that his brethren under his example and training might come to that place of torment. He was probably a professor of religion of the purest orthodoxy, but a man who loved the foremost dog in the chase more than he loved Lazarus. There are professors who love the dollar in their pocket more than they love the preacher who is taxing brain, body, and soul to preach for them and their families the unsearchable riches of Christ. Our Lord did not select the worst characters to show us who were lost, but those of fair reputation, and who could hold membership in any Church. It seems to us that those who are unbelievers in future endless punishment should seek to show that the term "hell" used here had the worst and not the best signification for the future state. Of course the body is not in torment, for it was very recently buried. If the soul can be in torment when it has only reached *hades*, what will be its condition when finally it reaches *hell?* As there is no intimation of the release of the rich man in all the centuries that have passed, let men measure and weigh their words when they fix a light meaning to the rich man's torment in the first hour of his misery.

Let us analyze the character of the rich man. As we have said, it was a *certain* rich man who was named, and not *any* rich man; therefore the real character of this rich man is to be considered without special reference to his riches. The fact that he was a rich man, in itself viewed, does not prove that he was religious or irreligious, but is simply part of the description, so that his hearers might know the man. The statement that he was clothed in purple and fine linen and fared sumptuously every day is for the purpose of identity and description, and not as explaining his character. If he had been a poor man living in a cottage, the same sins might be brought to his door that are chargeable to his account. One of the strongest sayings of the word of God as to riches is this: "The love of money is the root of all evil." Here the sin is not in having money, but it is in its inordinate love. A man without a dollar may love money so as to be guilty of this sin, while a millionaire may hold money with a light and easy hand and heart as a gift from his Lord to be used for his glory. In such a case the former is guilty of the sin named, and the latter is not only free from the guilt but so uses the mammon of unrighteousness as to do great good. It is true that riches often become a snare and a temptation to commit the sin of loving money; but this is the fault of the possessor of the riches, and not of the riches themselves. And every man possessing riches must watch and examine himself narrowly at this point.

What was the rich man's sin? In the absence of houses and homes prepared by law for the poor, it was the custom of the country to carry the unfortunate like Lazarus to the gates and doors of the rich and there leave them for the gratuitous gifts of bread and water which were expected to be bestowed by those in affluence. So far as the account goes we cannot find any greater sin in the rich man than allowing a poor man full of sores to lie unattended at his gate, and between his bodily sufferings and his hunger to die. Certainly this was a great sin; but it might happen in the nineteenth century, and in the Church of God. There is nothing in the account to indicate that it was miserliness on the part of the rich man that caused the sufferings and death of the poor man, but it was an act of unjustifiable neglect. The law of the land did not compel the rich man to feed Lazarus, hence we learn that God holds us responsible for some duties not expressly enjoined by law. Here is a man who has lost his soul, and his worst act is one not laid at his door by legal obligation. It might be supposed that the rich man did not know that Lazarus was at his gate; but when we remember the custom of the country, that his carriers were to lay him at the gate and give the rich man notice, connected with the humble and pleading petition of the poor man for the crumbs that fell from the rich man's table, and the immediate recognition of the poor man by the rich man after both were dead, we cannot doubt that the rich man knew his condition and wants, and purposed to attend to them, but was so absorbed in his pleasures and pursuits that they escaped his memory.

When we come to inquire further what was the sin of the rich man, we shall have to penetrate deeper than his external conduct. Doubtless there was many a time the whisper to his soul: "Ye shall not surely die. Look around and see the deeds of goodness on the part of God, and take courage against unnecessary alarm. Think of the summer and the sunshine, and the days of health allotted, and the fruits of the earth, and the flowers, and the friends, and the perpetual round of enjoyments, and dismiss all fears of hell." Storms, drought, epidemics, sickness, feebleness, age, and enemies are kept out of sight as suggestive arguments to show the severity of God.

Again, we have no information nor any fact recorded that creates a probability that this man ever truly repented of his sins. He regarded himself as quite moral and better than other men. Dividing society into classes, he considered himself as in the first list. The notion of total depravity of moral nature as applied to himself was a monstrous conception, and when the Scripture asserted, "The whole head is sick, and the whole heart is faint," it was not his head nor his heart that was meant.

He trusted in himself that he was righteous. Every good deed done for a neighbor was written down in his book as part of the reward which should enable him to enter heaven, but it had no place in the Lamb's book of life. He was afraid of the lightning and thunder which lasted only a moment, but was not afraid of hell which lasted forever.

His faith was no better than his repentance. While he read Moses and the prophets, and called Abraham his father, he saw only the deist's God. His eyes never beheld God or his Son as making propitiation for his sins. He had faith without perceiving the real object of faith. Being whole as he conceived, he did not see that he needed a physician. He had read of the balm of Gilead and the physician there, but did not realize that he needed the remedy. That to-morrow should "as this day be, and more abundant" for him, he had no doubt. The very day that he entered hell he said: "Soul, take thine ease; thou hast much goods laid up in store for many years." Many, many radical defects were in his character and filling him with sin because he had never prayed, "God be merciful to me a sinner!"

Here we have an exception to the rule that our knowledge of men stops at the grave. We attend them in their last sickness, minister to their wants, sympathize with their feebleness, forget their defects, magnify their virtues, and place almost implicit confidence in their last utterances. The most of men hope that they have made peace with God, and there is charity enough in the breasts of the survivors to believe that the hope is justified. Even in death-bed repentances perhaps it is well enough to hope for the best result, while we must know—if we allow ourselves to reason about it in the light of God's word, and from our observation of those who recover from sickness after all expectation of recovery is gone—that such professions of change of heart are very unreliable. No step is more unwise than to venture on a life of sin and impenitence trusting to forgiveness in the last hour. Let us take advantage of this rare opportunity, and enter eternity with one who has been dead in the body only a single hour.

Notice how soon the rich man is dead; and at the same moment he is in hell, in torment, in conscious misery extending to the very tip of his tongue, and realizing the past, present, and future of all his history and surroundings. He can now remember the word of the Lord, "The wicked shall be turned into hell, and all the nations that forget God." His condition is personally serious and critical, and there is no room for an account of associates around him in torments like his own. While his body lies still in death, the undertaker measuring him for the coffin, busy fingers preparing his shroud, the minister or other officiating person preparing the choicest eulogy on his worth and virtues, and probably his piety, instantly his spirit, with wondrous powers of increased capacity, views the whole scene of past misdirected influence, of present pain, and of future danger to himself and his brethren. His vision is so enlarged that he can see across the great gulf that is fixed from hell to heaven. His knowledge is so accurate that he can recognize Abraham who had lived and died many centuries before he came into the world. His hearing is so improved that he understands the words spoken by Abraham in heaven, although the tone is that of ordinary conversation. His voice can be heard in heaven from hell and the words plainly understood. The time is so short since he died that his human earthly feelings are all unchanged as he pleads for his brethren and prays for their welfare. Like a drowning man catching at straws, his prayer is to Abraham, as he is in his sight. What are we to think of his mental powers now after nineteen centuries have passed, when one hour showed such amazing strength? How do he and his brethren stand to-day related to eternity? Is it not well that the word eternity occurs but once in the Scriptures? One eternity for the good and one for the bad, but O how different!

In the true development of the rich man's character and that of other sinners dwelling in all the world like him, the most astounding statement is made to him by Abraham in the close of their colloquy: "If they hear not Moses and the prophets, neither would they be persuaded though one rose from the dead." Men take for granted two false positions—that God is under obligation to furnish more proof of his will and man's duty and the realities of eternity than he has furnished, and that such additional proof would lead all men to repentance.

In this life the Christian walks by faith and not by sight. If demonstrations of a mathematical kind, or proofs most obvious to his senses, were furnished every man of the torments of hell and the bliss of heaven, there would be no virtue in obedience to God, any more than we are not entitled to praise for keeping our hands out of the fire. We must act from principle and on reasonable faith on these subjects to merit any consideration for our course. Now God has furnished us the most abundant and most satisfactory evidence of which these subjects are capable. Constant miracles to prove every position would soon lose their force, and occasional miracles would be liable to imitation and deception. But when all revealed truth is contained in human language and comes to us under inspiration from heaven, and is capable of transfer to all the dialects of earth, we have proofs which no reasonable man may gainsay and which abide with us forever. And it is the climax of presumption for lost and sinful man to dictate to God in the least degree either the extent or manner of revelation which he shall make of his will to us.

The greatest hinderance to voluntary faith is in a disrelish of the things proposed. In religion the depraved heart dislikes the justice of God and the terms of his law, and therefore an opposition to the truth arises before the argument in its favor is considered. We say boldly that if the proofs of the Christian religion were addressed to mankind just as they are, and all natural desires led to the hope that they were true, there would not be an unbeliever found among men. The Christian religion is proved to be true by all the kinds and varieties of evidence, miracles, prophesy, internal conformity to man's best interests, history, and every degree of probability. But the universal cry of the depraved heart is, We will not have this man Christ Jesus to reign over us!

What a striking contrast appears at two points between the rich man and Lazarus! The rich man lay in purple and fine linen, attended by physicians, kindred, and neighbors, relieved from suffering as far as medicine and attention could relieve him, and when dead has a costly burial and funeral. The poor man died covered with sores and perishing with hunger, unburied, and unattended except by the dogs. In an hour the rich man is in hell and the poor man in heaven. The resources of God are infinite, and these men change places immediately. The rich man is painfully reminded that he had all his good things while alive and Lazarus his evil things, and that now their conditions are changed forever. Lazarus speaks not a word even of the rich man's neglect, while the rich man pleads as long as he can have an audience with Abraham.

We doubt whether any character in the Bible is presented with as little recorded of his good deeds as that of Lazarus, where it is certain that noble virtues were possessed. The heavenly registry will contain them all; the earthly registry may not know one of them. As the rich man is sent into endless torment without any specification of outward sins, so Lazarus reaches Abraham's bosom after a life so quiet that not one of its deeds was known. Humanly speaking, he appears the most passive of men, carried by beggars without a word of thankfulness or complaint, and only once making even a request, when in extreme hunger he asked for the crumbs that fell from the rich man's table. Let these thoughts destroy within us all hope that our works have such merit with God as to assist in our salvation to any degree. History is turned an unusual way in this instance, the antecedents of Lazarus being all unknown, and his unhonored death and blissful life beyond being written in undying letters. We believe that he had done many good deeds in the days of his health and strength, and that some will rise up in the judgment to call him blessed, but now they are among the secrets of the Lord. His life was of that kind that "tells no tale of all the good it does."

The name Lazarus has a significance: it signifies God is my help. There is no other name than the name Jesus "given under heaven among men whereby we must be saved." Through his name whosoever believeth in him shall receive remission of sins. At his name every knee shall bow and every tongue confess. And in the destitute and helpless condition of poor Lazarus it was a comfort to have a name that possessed in its very signification strong trust in God. The name has passed into many languages on account of the profound impression made on men by this parable. To one who has no overt acts of his life recorded in memory of his good works, it is well to have a name significant of religious virtue. May our name, dear reader, be written on the palms of the hands of the Redeemer!

The Jews, in our Saviour's day, named three places to which they supposed the righteous went when they died. They supposed that some went to the garden of Eden, some to be under the throne of glory, and some to the bosom of Abraham. They said that as Abraham was the father of the faithful it was eminently proper that the righteous Jews should go to him; and so our Lord here shows them that one of their own number who relied upon his own righteousness did not go to Abraham, but a poor beggar who could not receive the crumbs that fell from the rich man's table not only reached Abraham's bosom, but he was carried thither by the angels of God. Such expressions as the one here given, and such as "To-day shalt thou be with me in paradise," and others of a similar character used by our Lord, would strike the Jewish mind with great power. And we see that while Lazarus died so full of sores in his body that he was probably untouched by men and left without a burial, kind angels took charge of his spirit as a precious trust and bore it away to the realms of light and life.

We can easily tell the true character of Lazarus while living in the world by his condition after death. Very many scriptures assure us that none but those who live righteously can die and enter heaven. The kindred of Lazarus, the place where he lived, and his Church relations are all unknown, but that he had true repentance toward God and saving faith, accompanied with the Holy Spirit to regenerate his soul, and a life of obedience on his part, we know as well as if our Lord had given us in detail the religious experience and life of this good man. An abode in heaven is positive proof of faithfulness on earth. Very unsatisfactory must the reflection be to any man when he thinks soberly of any possible effort that he can make in a dying-hour to answer the demands of eternity with a life load of sin accumulated in the past. But to the saint who falls asleep in Jesus, how sweet the retrospect of a life devoted to his service, and how bright the prospect of entering heaven and dwelling forever with the Lord! Let the reader take choice between the examples set before him in the lives, death, and future condition of the rich man and Lazarus. "Do quickly what is in thine heart. The night cometh when no man can work."

THE RESURRECTION OF CHRIST.

"The Lord is risen indeed." Luke xxiv. 34.

IT has been said that for many years after "our Jesus had gone up on high," on each returning Sunday, which was the day of his resurrection, the Christian children in Jerusalem, and in many other places, were accustomed to wear badges on their garments having the words written on them in large and plain letters, "The Lord is risen indeed." What a beautiful procession would be thus formed by the young people who had given their hearts to Christ! In a period of persecution and danger courage mixed with faith would make the scene all the brighter.

These five words are the foundation, center, and superstructure of the Christian system. On them rests the Bible and all our hopes of immortality and heaven. If they are true, an abundant entrance will be ministered to the saints in light beyond the present pilgrimage; if they are false, more than Egyptian darkness settles down upon the world, and of all men the believers in them are most miserably duped. If they are false? Impossible! They are upheld by all the varieties of evidence; by history, by miracles, by prophecy; by the goodness of our Lord and the purity of his teachings; by the necessity of the case and by Christian experience. We propose to examine the subject as a *question of fact*, so that all men may look at the proofs alike and with impartial eyes, if they will.

The Jews and the Christians are the only people competent to examine and decide the question before us. Other nations believed in "lords many and gods many," and did not have the books, the inclination, or the opportunity, to understand our subject. It is one of the most remarkable things in the world that the Jews and Christians not only had an interest in the subject from opposite sides that led them to its most careful and thorough study, but they read the same books and relied on the same authorities. We defy the world to produce another controversy where the contending parties agreed on all the disputed questions except one. All the antecedent questions, such as the books to be received as canonical, the promise of a Messiah, the appearance, life, and death of Christ, with his asserted claims to Messiahship, are all admitted by both parties, and the issue is narrowed down to the question, *What became of the body* of Jesus after he was crucified and buried? Here is an agreement unparalleled, and an issue strange and wonderful. Both parties say that the body of Jesus was never seen *in death* after it was laid in the tomb of Joseph.

The Resurrection of Christ.

Two questions of importance demand attention: 1. Is there a book called the Bible which makes Jesus Christ, who is said to have risen from the dead, its central figure? 2. Was there such a man as Jesus Christ living in the age and at the places named, as stated in his life written by four historians?

1. The Bible. We *know* with certainty that there is such a book as the Bible. We have read it in our own native tongue. It consists of two parts called the Old and the New Testament. Jesus Christ was predicted in the first as the coming Saviour of the world, and in the last the history of his coming is made known. This book called the Bible has been translated into nearly all the dialects of earth, and its friends to-day are sending it to every part of the habitable globe with the claim of its inspiration from heaven. That claim secures its careful protection by its friends, and its critical scrutiny by its enemies. Let us look at it in the light of the question before us.

Some forty authors wrote the Bible. No human book has been written by so many pens except when this very Bible has demanded translation or revision. These authors were of every variety of ability, and yet on all the great subjects of the book which the world by searching never ascertained— such as God, man, salvation, the soul, worship, and our immortality—they not only substantially but literally agree. God must have moved the hands and hearts to write the words.

Again, fifteen hundred years elapsed from the writing of the first book to the last. The world was twenty-five hundred years old when the first book was written. God, by Moses, wrote the chief heads of doctrine and duty on stone to show that it was imperishable. No other book was ever fifteen hundred years in preparation, or perhaps more than one hundred years. Surely the Bible is the most wonderful of books, and deserves the most profound consideration.

It would be trifling with the intelligence of the world to doubt the existence of the Jews as a nation from a period as far back as profane history can reach. Their Bible, the Old Testament, was in their hands running back to the date of each book, and it is in their hands to-day. What are some of its contents? As a book governing the Jews, it contains their *genealogy*, their *laws*, and their *religion*.

All people are particular as to their *genealogy*. No truer account is found than the family record in our Bibles. Here births, deaths, and marriages are correct to a day. The subject is more important where the laws of primogeniture obtain. Every reason existed with the Jews for keeping an exact genealogy. Knowing, as the centuries passed, that they were the chosen people of God, and that they held his revealed truth, they were more careful to preserve their family record. Added to this they were divided into twelve tribes, which increased the value of a true history of each one. No mistake could possibly occur among them in their genealogical tables that would not be detected. Now these tables run through the Old Testament. They rest side by side with the prophecies which predict *our Christ*.

The *laws* of any country are so well known and so revered that forgery is impossible. Neither a general nor a local law could be passed on any people as their own law unless they had received it as such. All the courts would reject it at once. The Jewish Scriptures contain the civil and penal laws of the Jews. When additions were made they were made through the additional Scriptures that were given to them by inspiration. Plato, a heathen, said, "No mortal can make laws to purpose;" and Demosthenes said "law was the inspiration and gift of God." Running along side by side with the prophecies which predict the coming of *our Christ* are the laws of the Jews. From Moses to John the Baptist, destruction, mutilation, or change of these laws would be an absolute impossibility. The Jewish genealogy and laws were kept intact throughout the centuries, and these stood as a high wall protecting every prophecy that referred to our Lord.

A people situated as were the Jews would be

tenaciously jealous of their *religion*. Indeed, all people are sensitive at this point. The destruction of an idol-temple has been the cause of war. But the Jews had received the holy law from God; he had talked to their prophets and seers, he had been a pillar of cloud by day and a pillar of fire by night, and he was always to them as the shadow of a great rock in a weary land. He had prohibited idolatry, and had given them a pure, spiritual worship. Hence in their darkest day they had more than seven thousand men who had not bowed the knee to Baal.

The pertinency of these truths, as applied to the resurrection of our Saviour, is seen in the fact that the most bitter enemies of the cross, the Jews, furnish scriptures full of prophecy that present the Lord as truly and circumstantially as if they had been writing his life after his decease. Some infidels have felt the weight of the prophetical argument until they have raised the question whether the Jewish Scriptures were not written after our Lord's advent into the world. All the proof is overwhelming that the last of the Old Testament Scriptures was written four hundred years before the birth of Christ, and the first of them fifteen hundred years before that time. Now we aver that one hundred Scriptures, or more, written between the periods named, present our Lord with prehistoric faithfulness. The idle dream of Lord

THE RESURRECTION OF CHRIST. 237

Bolingbroke that Christ and his friends made his life to conform to the prophecies that they might thereby secure a triumph, is too absurd to be considered. He is the only infidel who has risked his reputation on such a statement. Could they choose the place and time of the birth of Jesus, his flight into Egypt, his miracles, his betrayal, his death, and his resurrection, to secure a triumph? Let us notice a few of the prophecies concerning our Lord made centuries before he was born.

We read in Micah, written seven hundred years before Christ: "But thou, Bethlehem-Ephratah, though thou be little among the thousands of Judah, yet out of thee shall he come forth unto me that is to be ruler in Israel; whose goings forth have been from of old, from everlasting." In Matthew we read that Jesus was born in Bethlehem of Judea, and the prophecy above was applied to him in these words: "And thou, Bethlehem, in the land of Juda, art not the least among the princes of Juda; for out of thee shall come a Governor, that shall rule my people Israel." At that moment the wise men of the East were believers in Jesus, and Herod the king was troubled about him, so that a demonstration exists as soon as he was born that he was the Messiah foretold in prophecy.

In Hosea we read: "When Israel was a child, then I loved him and called my son out of Egypt." This prediction was made seven hundred and forty years before Christ. No human sagacity could foresee that Christ would be born in Bethlehem, and that in consequence of a cruel decree of Herod to slay all the male children in Judea of two years old and under, the parents of Jesus would select Egypt as the country to which they would flee, and that the historian of our Lord would use it as the fulfillment of this prophecy, saying, "Out of Egypt have I called my son."

One thousand years before our Lord was born the psalmist made this prophecy concerning him: "They part my garments among them, and cast lots upon my vesture." At the crucifixion this was fulfilled. The history says: "And they crucified him, and parted his garments, casting lots; that it might be fulfilled which was spoken by the prophet, They parted my garments among them, and upon my vesture did they cast lots."

We need not quote more specific prophecies concerning Jesus which had fulfillment either in his life or death. His life, death, and resurrection are full of them. Whole chapters of Isaiah may be read as the history of Jesus Christ, and they were written seven hundred years before he was born into the world. The argument from prophecy is undoubted proof that Jesus was the Son of God. It is only resisted where the mind and heart are set on unbelief.

Was there such a man as Jesus Christ? It seems

unnecessary to ask the question. But its importance exists in the fact that if he really lived the works done by him required the power of God to do them, and if he was a mythical person there were abundant witnesses to prove the fact. When four separate histories were published throughout the land shortly after his crucifixion and resurrection, the Christian religion would have been crushed by showing that its author was an imaginary person. Hannibal and Cæsar and the first Napoleon lived no more certainly than did Jesus Christ. Josephus, Suetonius, and Tacitus all mention Christ, the latter recording at length the progress of his religion; and no one ever thought of disputing the accuracy of these histories. About one hundred and thirty years after the ascension of our Lord, the astute infidel Celsus wrote against Christianity, in which all the main facts of the life of Christ were stated and admitted. He was answered by Origen. Next, Porphyry, in the third century, did the same thing, making the same admissions. To this day infidels acknowledge that Christ lived.

We come now to the life of our Lord. He was a "man of sorrows and acquainted with grief." His enemies despised even the town where he was brought up, saying, "Can any thing good come out of Nazareth?" His lowly origin and life were their chief hope of his defeat. Tantalizingly they said: "He is only the son of a carpenter, and his mother and kindred are all here with us—plain, common people, having no prestige, and nothing on which to found the belief that he was to be the Messiah." Such was his appearance to all men as he entered upon the active stage of life.

No man is obliged to prove a negative. It is not required in any court. But all experience and observation show that all men will establish the negative of any proposition where they can easily do so, and where by that proof their adversary will be vanquished. Let us apply this statement to Christ. Romans and Jews and all the public authorities, with the influence of public and private opinion, stood ready to oppose the claims of our Lord. He was without worldly power or influence. The design of his life required the greatest publicity. It was to convince the world that he was sent by the Father to redeem the world. He did nothing in a corner. As we have shown, his birth made such an impression that it drew the wisdom of the world through the wise men of the East to the place of his nativity, and caused the destruction of many infants under the decree of Herod. If either had not occurred as stated, the fact was capable of proof by the enemies of Christ, and would have been sufficient to silence his cause forever.

John the Baptist, the forerunner of Jesus, prepared his way in the most public manner. "Jerusalem, and all Judea, and all the region round about Jordan" attended his preaching, and were baptized of him. In the midst of this universal repentance and reformation Jesus appeared publicly and was baptized by John, and the heavens were opened, and the Spirit in the form of a dove sat upon Jesus, and a voice was heard proclaiming, "This is my beloved Son, in whom I am well pleased." How easy to disprove such public acts, if they had not taken place!

The miracles of Christ were of the most public and notorious kind. They were performed for three years. Enemies and friends saw them and were the subjects of their relief. All the hatred of earth could make no better explanation than this: "He casts out devils by Beelzebub, the prince of the devils." The daughter of Jairus, the son of the widow of Nain, and Lazarus were raised from death in the sight of believers and unbelievers. When infidels say Christ should have appeared to his enemies after his resurrection to convince them of the fact, the answer is that if they would not believe on him seeing these three notable instances of raising the dead, neither would they believe if they had witnessed his own resurrection. Five thousand people were fed when the visible supply was only a few loaves and fishes. The blind saw, the deaf heard, and the dumb talked, whenever he willed it. In city and town and country place these great works occurred. Clay and spittle were the strongest medicinal preparations seen or used at any time. Usually the work was done by a word of command. With what alacrity his enemies would have shown by the thousands present at the miracles that none of these great works took place, if they had been a delusion or an imposition!

Consider the day of Pentecost. By this time the main question of the resurrection of Christ had been agitated for nearly two months. The place was Jerusalem, where the Lord had been sentenced to death, and in whose suburbs he had been crucified, and from thence ascended on high, leading captivity captive. On the day of Pentecost a most notable miracle took place. The Christians then present, numbering one hundred and twenty, and the most of them plain and unlearned persons, were enabled by divine power to speak in every tongue then known. This they did in the hearing of the thousands who were present, representing many nationalities, so that every one heard their testimony for Jesus in his own speech. Then followed a sermon by Peter, setting forth the facts that Jesus had been crucified by them, that he had risen from the dead only a few weeks before the sermon was preached, and that he was their Redeemer. As many as three thousand people on that day heard, believed, and obeyed the gospel. Now, if all this had been written down in the Acts of the Apostles shortly after the time when these great events were alleged to have occurred, and they were all a fiction, how easy by the testimony of thousands of people to demonstrate their falsehood! But all that the authorities did was to command them to teach no more in the name of Jesus, and sometimes to imprison the boldest Christians.

As the crucifixion of Jesus drew nigh, and when it had actually occurred, the confederate powers who sought by his death to destroy every vestige of pretension that he was the Messiah are found in each step taken adding to the proof of his Messiahship until all possible doubts are removed. Their publicity established his claim. Their persecution showed his goodness and love. Their hatred gave power to his prayers. Their malice demonstrated his meekness. Hell and earth became blind to their interest, while heaven shone upon the world with immortal luster.

Mark the trial of Christ. He stands without counsel or witnesses. No one pleads for him or cross-examines a single man giving testimony. The judges cry out the sentence in open court without consultation with each other. They are seeking his life, but they desire the protection of the forms of law. The sentence is determined. Pontius Pilate hesitates, and then yields and signs the death-warrant. Jesus is taken out to Calvary and crucified. A hooting mob and rabble of probably fifteen hundred people attend the scene. While he is dying he speaks seven times with heavenly kindness so that his murderers can hear him. He dies. It is on Friday. He is laid in the tomb of Joseph of Arimathea. Jews, Romans, sinners, enemies, strangers, and citizens have in their control all the power of earth as against Jesus. Friday, Saturday, Sunday morning are the time noted. He predicted that he would rise from the dead the third day.

We now reach the issue made between Jews and Christians. What became of the body of Christ on the third day after he was crucified and buried?

Our Lord had attracted the most public and marked attention in the presence of Jews, Romans, and Christians for a period of three years before his death, during which time he claimed to be the Messiah, and predicted not only his death, but also his resurrection on the third day after his death. All this is exceedingly important, as showing the advantages it gave his enemies to prevent collusion and fraud as to his body on the third day, and to enable them to detect any manner of imposture that might exist. What is the history of the third day?

Within two miles of Jerusalem—a city full of inhabitants and strangers at the time, numbering in all nearly a million of souls; where there was a police and military force of many hundreds, all in the hands of the enemies of the Lord; not beyond the suburbs, where the population was necessarily dense—early in the morning after daylight there was lying in a new tomb, wherein man had never before been laid, a dead man named Jesus Christ; which tomb was sealed with the seal of State, and to break which seal was punishable with death, and around which tomb was a guard of one hundred soldiers—if a Roman centurion's company, or sixty-four if a Jewish watch—to each one of whom death was the penalty if found asleep: when suddenly the body of this dead man was missing, and neither friends nor foes claim that it was ever seen afterward as a dead body. What became of that precious body?

Hear first the enemies of our Lord. They do not pretend that any of their soldiers arrested any one for taking the body, or attempted any arrest, or even a discovery. As against themselves they admit their soldiers were asleep, the punishment for which offense was death to each one. The hour when they made the discovery of the missing body was the first hour, when it was necessary for the soldiers to remain awake during the three preceding days, and was the first hour of the third day, the day predicted by the Lord for his resurrection. An arrest or discovery of the thief would have saved the soldiers' lives, and would have proved the claims of Jesus to be false. They do not pretend that they had posted any sentinels. The soldiers went immediately to the city after the body was missing and reported the strange history to the authorities. A hundred search-warrants to find the body could have been issued in an hour, and five hundred officers sent in search of it, and the whole country could have been aroused to help make the discovery. There were no railroads or other rapid means of conveyance to carry it away. Not a move was made to find the body. The soldiers knew and reported the fact that the body was supernaturally removed, and this was the reason that no discovery was attempted. The friends of the Lord were affrighted almost to death, and were as sheep without a shepherd. Suppose there were no other proof, is there any evidence against any man or body of men, which could be believed for a moment, that they stole the body? The conviction is irresistible that the authorities knew the tale was false from their own conduct in failing to try to prove it was true.

The thinnest fabrication ever made was the one invented on that third day morning to account for the missing body. It was that while the soldiers slept the disciples came by night and stole it away. The lowest magistrate's court in the United States would not allow a witness to testify to a supposed event that occurred while he acknowledged himself to be asleep. If they were asleep, for aught that they knew to the contrary, Jesus may have risen from the dead. Breaking the seal and removing the stone and the body would certainly awake some of the soldiers. The body could have been found if it had been stolen, but the attempt was not made. No company of soldiers would all have slept at once when death was the penalty.

Hear the friends of Jesus. There was never a word of suspicion uttered against the moral integrity of the disciples, who asserted that they saw him alive on the third day and afterward. To be alive and to rise from the dead, if he were the Messiah, would be in exact fulfillment of the Scriptures received by his enemies, and of his own recent prediction. The power of God to accomplish the end was undoubtedly sufficient.

The importance to the Christian religion cannot be overestimated that our Lord should furnish proof that he was alive on the very day of his resurrection. A day later, or a week later, and the whole infidel world would have said there was time for collusion. How much proof is there of his being seen alive on the first day? He appeared to Mary Magdalene and the other Mary soon after he was risen from the tomb (Matt. xxviii. 9). Then he appeared to the two disciples on their way to Emmaus (Mark xvi. 12). On the same day he appeared to the eleven as they sat at meat (Mark xvi. 14). He also appeared to Simon Peter, who had denied him (Luke xxiv. 34). Here were sixteen credible witnesses who knew Jesus well, to whom he appeared on the first day of his resurrection.

The attack made on their proof is that they were friends. This is all. Their moral character is unimpeached. After this day, for several weeks our Lord often appeared alive, at one time to more than five hundred persons. Would not any sane man believe such testimony, as opposed to the weakness of the other side, in any case where he was not prejudiced? On the one side there is positive proof by more than five hundred witnesses to a plain fact that they knew and saw with their eyes; on the other side the proof is offered of a supposed event occurring while the witnesses acknowledged they were asleep, and which testimony was given to make large sums of money and to save their own lives.

Two events show the abiding conviction of the civilized world that Jesus rose from the dead. One is that the date used in all official and private transactions before that time had commenced and run from the creation of the world, but in honor of our Lord for nearly two thousand years all dates in all civilized countries are recorded from the birth of Christ. Every infidel who writes only a common letter to a friend must recognize the Saviour so far as to date his epistle in the year of our Lord corresponding with the date of his birth.

Again, the seventh day of the week had been the Jewish Sabbath in the past centuries before Christ, but since he ascended on high the first day of the week is recognized by civilized nations as the day of rest. Such honors have not been conferred upon any or all of the battles gained by all military heroes. These changes were made without express command in the Bible to make them, and are therefore stronger proof of the unchanging belief of the world that the claim is true that Christ has risen from the dead.

> The Lord is risen indeed:
>   He lives to die no more;
> He lives the sinner's cause to plead,
>   Whose curse and shame he bore.
>
> Then wake your golden lyres,
>   And strike each cheerful chord;
> Join, all ye bright, celestial choirs,
>   To sing our risen Lord.

THE END.

www.ingramcontent.com/pod-product-compliance
Lightning Source LLC
Chambersburg PA
CBHW020801230426
43666CB00007B/795